Why Fret
THAT
GOD
Stuff?

Learn to Let Go *and*
Let God Take Control

COMPILED BY

KATHY COLLARD MILLER

STARBURST PUBLISHERS, INC.

To schedule Author appearances write: Author Appearances, Starburst Promotions, P.O. Box 4123 Lancaster, Pennsylvania 17604 or call (717) 293-0939

Website: www.starburstpublishers.com

CREDITS:
Cover design by David Marty Design
Text design and composition by John Reinhardt Book Design

Unless otherwise noted, or paraphrased by the author, all Scripture quotations are from the New International Version of The Holy Bible.

"Scripture taken from the HOLY BIBLE: NEW INTERNATIONAL VERSION®. NIV®. Copyright © 1973, 1978, 1984 by International Bible Society. Used by permission of Zondervan Publishing House."

"The "NIV" and "New International Version" trademarks are registered in the United States Patent and Trademark Office by International Bible Society."

To the best of its ability, Starburst Publishers® has strived to find the source of all material. If there has been an oversight, please contact us and we will make any correction deemed necessary in future printings. We also declare that to the best of our knowledge all material (quoted or not) contained herein is accurate, and we shall not be held liable for the same.

First Printing, November, 1998

ISBN: 0-914984-50-0
Library of Congress Catalog Number 98-86025
Printed in the United States of America

Contents

Frustrating Circumstances

God's Ways

A Lack Of Faith

Failure

Finances

Marriage

Children

Relationships

Time Pressures

Wrong Attitudes

Prayer

Introduction

We all say we're going to stop worrying. We may often comment that fretting about life doesn't make things better, so why do we do it? We all feel unpleasant emotions like fear, dislike and distrust. We know God can help us diminish those reactions, yet it's hard sometimes to always respond like we should.

If you'd like some encouragement and inspiration to give you a boost toward greater trust in God, absence of fear and worry, plus wonderfully positive thoughts to create a great day, then *Why Fret That God Stuff?* is just the book for you!

Within the pages of this book, you'll find stories from the famous and the not-so-famous as they share their own struggles and how God assisted them to have more spiritual attitudes. Whether you read one of these heartening stores each morning or evening, or digest several at a time, you'll find your heart trusting God more and your mind thinking God's thoughts.

We really know we can trust God for everything! Find here an abundance of reasons for solidifying your faith in our awesome Lord!

KATHY COLLARD MILLER

Why Fret Waking With Joy?

RUTH E. MCDANIEL

The visiting minister stood at the pulpit, pointed at the congregation, and asked, "What kind of a Christian are you? Some people wake up in the morning and say, 'Good morning, Lord!' while others open sleepy eyes and moan, 'Good Lord! Morning!' Which category fits you?" I sank lower in my seat, knowing I was among the latter.

The pastor continued. "David was a man after God's own heart. Psalm 5:3 says he prayed first thing in the morning and we know he prayed enthusiastically because 'rejoice' is used repeatedly throughout his psalms.

"Obviously, David was a 'Good morning, Lord!' sort of guy who knew that starting your day on a positive note was essential to living a godly life. Just think of the effect a cheerful disposition would have on your fellow man. What a Christian witness! I challenge each of you to start your mornings with glad greetings to the Lord, followed by a time of prayer and fellowship. You'll see what a difference it makes."

It was a challenge I couldn't refuse. But, could I do it? For as long as I can remember, I've had a hard time getting up in the morning. And, now, I was supposed to hail the Lord with a joyful greeting? I was doubtful but determined to give it a try.

That night as I prayed, I asked God to help me greet Him cheerfully the next morning. Eventually, I fell asleep and, seemingly within minutes, it was time to get up. An automatic groan started low in my throat, then stopped. In awe, I heard myself say, "Good morning, Lord!" I did it! Or, rather, God did it! My lips curved in a smile as I finished my morning prayers, got dressed, and was ready to face the world in record time—with an upbeat attitude!

The pastor was right! What a difference it makes to greet people with a smile on your face and the love of God in your heart. The whole day went better.

Since then, it's become a habit to rejoice in the Lord the moment my eyes open. At last, I feel like I'm presenting a true Christian image. What about you? What kind of Christian are you? Does your fretting begin immediately when you wake? Change it to rejoicing!

In the morning, O LORD, you hear my voice; in the morning I lay my requests before you and wait in expectation.

Psalm 5:3

Why Fret Stupid Drivers?

DORIS STERNER YOUNG

"There they go again," I muttered to myself, "cutting me off. I don't know which is worse, cutting me off in traffic or following too closely." This encounter reminded me of other things drivers do that really annoy me. Things like not using turn signals, driving with high beams on, going too fast or going too slow. I wondered if there was a driver anywhere who didn't anger me in one way or another.

Even drivers at the self service gas station got under my skin. Especially the ones who took their time pulling away after their tanks were filled. I remembered wanting to yell something nasty at the woman who filled her tank, then got into her car and took the curlers out of her hair before driving off. If that didn't give me the right to be angry what would? After all she knew I was waiting to use that pump.

Arriving home still smarting from driver abuse, I picked up the ringing phone to find my friend, Marty, on the other end.

"What's wrong?" she asked when she heard my voice quivering.

"I just came home from a trip to the grocery store and I need to tell you there are some very stupid drivers out there." I gave her the litany of offenses that were fresh in my mind. "I came close to saying something mean to them."

"I have an expression you can say to them when you get upset behind the wheel," she replied.

Expecting some kind of zinger, I could hardly wait to hear what it might be.

"God bless you," she said.

"God bless you," I echoed in disbelief. "How is that going to help?" Before the question was out of my mouth I realized what a stupid one it was.

"Of course it helps," she said, "a blessing given is a blessing received. It begins by having a calming effect on our hearts and on our blood pressure. Most important, it helps us see others as children of God. As such they deserve our love not our hatred."

Marty passed away shortly after our talk but her wisdom lives on in my heart. She shares the driver's seat with me as I joyfully shout, "God Bless You," out my window to all the drivers who annoy me.

This is my command: Love each other.

John 15:17

Why Fret Middle Age Spread?

CINDY BAILEY

I noticed my skirt was a little snug one morning when I dressed for church. "Middle-aged spread," I muttered to myself as I looked in the mirror. "After all, I am turning forty this year. Can't look like a twenty-year-old forever."

Yet I couldn't help feeling kind of crotchety. All morning during worship I could think of nothing but how much the ravages of age were catching up with me.

After church, we had lunch with my husband's father who is nearly 80 and widowed these last five years. I sat brooding over my plate as I listened to him tell about his week. On Monday he led tours at our local museum. Tuesday was his day for visiting shut-ins. Thursday found him handing out coffee and donuts at the Christian outreach center. Saturday morning he met with the Boy Scouts to clear brush on a hiking trail. Of course on Sunday, he taught the fourth and fifth graders their Bible stories and worshipped the Lord with gladness.

Although he retired from forty-two years of teaching elementary school almost two decades ago and has been widowed for five years, it became oh-so-clear to me that his service for the Lord prevented him from fretting about getting old. His joy in the Lord was like a balm for my creaky joints, and I felt myself relaxing. Maybe it was time for me to quit sulking and respond to God's call to obey Him.

I never had "Mr. Bailey" for a teacher, yet he surely inspired me that day as much as any of his students, because his life is a lesson in faith. I have so much to learn from him about serving instead of fretting.

He seldom reflects on the days of his life, because God keeps him occupied with gladness of heart.

Ecclesiastes 5:20

Why Fret A Grudge?

LUIS PALAU

My father died when I was only 10 years old. I still remember hiding in someone's truck so I could go to the burial. No one thought children should attend such things. I dodged between people's legs so I could throw the first clump of dirt on my dad's casket.

Dad left us quite a bit of property and some money. But his four brothers squandered everything we had. In three years my family was living in poverty and debt.

When I was older and really understood what they had done, I urged my mother to take revenge by getting a lawyer and taking them to court. The older I became, the more bitter I grew. I learned that fretting the difficult experiences of life directly affected my spiritual well-being.

My mother always quoted verses that said to let God take revenge. She completely forgave my uncles for what they had done even though it took us twenty years to pay our debts. She simply refused to become bitter. She forgot what they had done. Consequently, God gave her a spirit free from fretting and many opportunities to serve Him.

I have seen as many lives spoiled by bitterness and a lack of forgiveness as by almost anything in the world. People experience physical and emotional breakdowns because they refuse to forgive others. My mother's example has inspired me to let God fulfill His justice, rather than fretting about trying to hand out revenge myself. I learned the longer I carry a grudge, the heavier it becomes. I cannot afford to harbor bitterness in my soul. As a result, I've experienced that same freedom and fruitfulness of my mother because I also forgave my uncles.

Do not take revenge, my friends, but leave room for God's wrath, for it is written: "It is mine to avenge, I will repay," says the Lord.

Romans 12:19

Why Fret Tithing?

KITTY BUCHOLTZ

"John, good news! I found a place that pays $50 for plasma. If I did that once a week, we'd have enough to pay all the bills."

My husband sighed. "You mean we're down to selling our blood?" He turned away and shook his head "No."

I had fretted over our finances for hours, trying to find a way to pay everything, perhaps subconsciously believing I could worry money into existence. It happened like this so often. John and I would act in haste without praying and soon we were in debt again.

Eight years later, we were so far in debt we filed for bankruptcy.

Looking back at those years, I now see a pattern. John and I would make a poor decision and money would get tight, so we would reduce spending and stop tithing. But circumstances often got worse.

Eventually, the situation would turn around, but then the cycle would begin again. Obviously, we made a lot of mistakes. But when we continued tithing, it felt like our finances improved more quickly. When we stopped tithing, it seemed our problems—and the emotional stress—lasted so much longer.

Recently, we were in the midst of another financial mini-crisis when I thought again about cutting back on our tithe for a while. Then I came across a passage in Malachi about tithing where God says, "Test me in this."

We prayed God would provide for our bills *and* our tithe, or show us that we misunderstood this Bible passage. As a result, God showed us a way out of our trouble *and* gave us an opportunity to increase our giving!

God doesn't ask all of us to serve Him in the same ways and He doesn't give us the same blessings. But John and I are certain we heard Him calling us to trust Him to provide for our needs and to be generous with His gifts. It's not easy, but trusting God is still far easier than fretting. I think I'll do well to remember that when the next crisis comes along.

"Bring the whole tithe into the storehouse, that there may be food in my house. Test me in this," says the Lord Almighty, "and see if I will not throw open the floodgates of heaven and pour out so much blessing that you will not have room enough for it."

Malachi 3:10

Why Fret Impossibilities?

C. LOUISE BROOKS

The pastor asked if it was anyone's birthday!

Small blonde curls bobbed as he stood on his proud daddy's knee waving his hand.

"How old are you today Caleb?" the Pastor inquired.

"Two. Two yeaws olt! It's my birt-day!" He turned to face us, holding up his two tiny fingers. The church burst out in joyous praise and clapping. He was our miracle baby!

When Caleb's family started attending our church, he was two months old and had been in the hospital since birth. As a preemie, he lay in the incubator fighting for his life. He came into this world 20 weeks after conception, weighing only 1 pound and 14 ounces. His chances of survival were worse than that of a baby bird that had fallen out of its nest. But his parents believed in a healing God and they brought their faith to us, requesting prayer.

Preemies go through many stages of crises. Caleb was no exception. The digestive system wasn't working right. Then, the doctor said he needed to be strong enough to get off the oxygen. Next, there was a possibility of blindness.

At each turning point, by faith we prayed and God powerfully interceded!

Today, Caleb is celebrating his second birthday! Preemies are not supposed to progress as well as full-term babies. But Caleb is healthy and normal. With his blonde locks of hair forming a soft halo around his face and his intelligent, blue eyes shining as if God Himself had lit them with starlight, we know God has completed His work.

Caleb was given little hope by the world's standards, but because we stood in the gap with prayer each time a crisis arose, God completed him!

Can a miracle like this relate to our everyday problems? God has not chosen to instantly make our entire day, or week, or year perfect! But the Father has taught us, through Caleb, to put each situation before Him—as it comes! He will complete each day, just as He perfectly completed Caleb. Not all at once, but one step at a time!

This is the confidence we have in approaching God: that if we ask anything according to his will, he hears us.

1 John 5:14

Why Fret Obedience?

DOUG SCHMIDT

The story is told of a young Christian farmer in search of land who came across forty acres strewn with boulders, tree stumps, and thistles. The price was right, however, so he bought the field and got to work. Throughout the winter the young man cleared all the debris from the land. By the time spring rolled around, he was ready to plant.

On a bright day in April, the new pastor in town came by to compliment the farmer on his hard work.

"I understand that this field used to be an eyesore for the folks around here. Looks like you and the Lord did a great job clearing it."

"Yes," said the young man, "but you should have seen it before I started helping the Lord out."

That anecdote can make us question, "What does it really mean to leave something in the Lord's hands? Do we just step back and do nothing but pray?"

If we've taken every appropriate action, or we're facing something that is totally beyond our control, then the answer is unequivocally *yes!*—prayer is the only remaining option.

As a believer, the young farmer appreciated the fact that his knowledge of farming and his physical strength came from God.

He also knew, however, that God expected him to obey and use those gifts . . . not to just sit on them and wait for the Lord to act as a demonstration of his "faith."

What does it mean to leave something in the Lord's hands? We must repeatedly ask ourselves, "What is the next, most responsible thing I can do?"—and then do it accompanied by prayer. When the only remaining option is to pray, then it's time to let go and simply trust God with the results.

The Lord said, "Shall I hide from Abraham what I am about to do? . . . For I have chosen him, so that he will direct his children and his household after him to keep the way of the LORD by doing what is right and just, so that the LORD will bring about for Abraham what he has promised him."

Genesis 18:17, 19

Why Fret Physical Handicaps?

J. OSWALD SANDERS

In 1939 it was my privilege to visit one of God's great noblewomen, Hannah Higgens of Melbourne, Australia. For sixty-nine of her eighty-two years she had been in constant pain as the result of a progressive bone disease that ultimately required the amputation of both arms and legs. Yet in her "cage" she would "sit and sing to Him who placed her there." She named her cottage "Gladwish." And for forty-three years she lived in one room.

How easy it would have been for her to give up the struggle and relapse into an orgy of self-pity. Instead, she accepted her limitations and acted on her God-given ministry to share with other invalids the love and comfort of God that had been her portion.

She had an attachment fixed to the stump of her right arm that enabled her to write with a fountain pen. It takes little imagination to understand the physical effort she had to exert when writing, since she had to use her whole body to form each character. As I write, I have before me one of her letters in the almost flawless script she learned to write.

Hannah's little room became a place of pilgrimmage for people from all over the world. From it went thousands of letters to visitors and fellow sufferers worldwide, which produced a rich harvest of blessing. The walls of her room were covered with photographs of correspondents to whom she had ministered and in many cases had led to the Lord. Of her it could be truly said that she turned her trouble into treasure and her sorrow into song.

Though the fig tree does not bud and there are no grapes on the vines, though the olive crop fails and the fields produce no food, though there are no sheep in the pen and no cattle in the stalls, yet I will rejoice in the LORD, I will be joyful in God my Savior.

Habakkuk 3:17–18

(Page 54, *Facing Loneliness*, by J. Oswald Sanders, Discovery House, MI, 1988. Used by permission.)

Why Fret The Darkness?

GAIL GAYMER MARTIN

Something about darkness is frightening even for adults. We look over our shoulders and flinch at strange noises. We lock our doors as the sun sets and peek out our windows at eerie sounds. We're frightened by our own unexpected shadow or reflection in a window.

In the darkness, we head for our automobiles in parking lots, alert and ready to defend ourselves. Coming home to a darkened house leaves us wary. Familiar things become strangely unfamiliar. We lose perspective. We bang our shins on table corners. Shadows and sounds are suspect.

About fifteen years ago, I went through an unwanted divorce. During the day, I felt miserable, but at night, I felt worse, alone and scared and hopeless. I sat on my bed, my night light glowing nearby, and talked out loud to God, asking Him to give me some little sign that my life would once again feel complete and happy.

I feel foolish now, thinking back. God had given me every "sign" I needed. All I had to do was read the Bible and believe. But instead, I fretted and tried to solve my problems alone. I laugh now, thinking of the wonderful way God helped me to grow and fill my life. God made my life better in these past years than I could ever have imagined.

Whether it is day or night, God's night light glows for all of us in the form of His love and grace. God's love chases away the shadows and loneliness, the fears and frustrations. He cares for us like the loving Father He has promised to be.

By day the LORD directs his love, at night his song is with me—a prayer to the God of my life.

Psalms 42:8

Why Fret The Weariness?

NANCY E. PETERSON

My son David attended a private Christian school six miles from our house and there was no bus service. I was driving to the school to pick him up every day and I was becoming more weary of it. In addition, my brother and I weren't getting along, Mom was sick, we had money problems, and my blood pressure was up.

I prayed, "Lord, I feel so angry at my brother and I'm tired of driving David. I'm worried about Mom and our financial situation. I know my anger is wearing me down to where I don't think I can go on. Why do I always have to deal with everything alone because my husband is working so many hours? I know he's trying to meet our financial needs, but I still feel angry."

During my prayer I felt ashamed and selfish. My brother probably was being difficult because he was having problems of his own. Mom didn't feel good, either, but she hardly ever complained. My husband worked so hard all the time, but he did it willingly because he loves us and wants to provide for us. Worse of all, I was selfish to be upset about a lack of money when we live in wealth compared to people in many parts of the world. As these thoughts occurred to me, I felt God must really be mad at me for my self-centeredness. Suddenly a song I hadn't heard in years started running through my head.

"Thou, O Lord, are a shield about me, You're my glory, You're the lifter of my head."

I knew He was telling me He understands when I get tired. I may start fretting about areas of my life, but He'll be my shield against letting it conquer me.

As I hummed that song, I felt refreshed. My circumstances weren't going to change immediately, but I knew God was in it with me. Suddenly, sharing honestly with God about my fretful feelings had lifted my spiritual "head." God still loved me! He wasn't even upset with me! What a glorious relief!

In that moment, I knew for sure God loved me because he infused me with His strength by helping me lift my spiritual attitude.

But you are a shield around me, O LORD; you bestow glory on me and lift up my head.

Psalm 3:3

Why Fret Moving?

DORIS SCHUCHARD

It was our first Christmas after a move that took us halfway across the country from family and friends. We decided to drive to a nearby farm and cut our own Christmas tree. Perhaps carrying on a family tradition would make me feel more at home.

Trudging through the frozen fields, our children spotted the perfect tree—long needled, fragrant and full, with a bird nest as an extra bonus. We took a family picture of our prize catch and loaded it onto the car roof.

The farmer's wife walked over to lend us a hand. "Could you use any boughs?" she inquired.

Looking at our bushy tree, I was about to reply we had more than enough greenery to decorate our house. But I stopped mid-sentence and followed her gaze as she pointed to a row of bright red "bows" hanging on a wall. Even something as simple as an accent made me feel I'd landed on another planet. I wondered if I'd ever be at home here.

I remembered the day months earlier when my husband announced, "It's an offer I can't turn down." So here I was, unloading my boxes of memories—each student's face I taught, friends who saw me through a debilitating disease, and grandma rocking my babies on creaky wooden floors. And what did I have to replace them with? Getting lost on the way to the grocery store, finding a doctor before the first child got sick, and not having a friend to list "in case of emergency."

On the move for forty years, the people of Israel who had been freed from Egyptian slavery seemed to voice my own fears, "Why did you bring us here, God? We would have rather remained in our former home. You brought us out to this wilderness to die." God quietly answered their cries by feeding, sheltering, and guiding His children on the long journey to their new home.

If God can move a whole nation, He will answer my longings, too. What remains behind in a move is only a physical framework and a geographical location. God is the true homebuilder. He travels ahead of me, preparing each new place for my habitation. As long as the Homebuilder dwells within, I can be at peace. Wherever God leads, I am home.

And if I go and prepare a place for you, I will come back and take you to be with me that you also may be where I am.

John 14:3

Why Fret Panic?

EDNA WELCH

In 1990, my husband and I, retired school teachers, joined in a project sponsored by the Southern Baptist Convention and the People's Republic of China to teach English to Chinese teachers in Mainland China. We were to spend six weeks there.

After orientation training in Los Angeles and Hong Kong, we were making our way through the Hong Kong train terminal, anticipating traveling to our assignment. Never had we seen so many people jammed together in one space who did not speak English. I began to feel nervous. This quickly changed to extreme anxiety when the luggage cart my husband, Jim, was pushing, got caught in the escalator. He fell, then I fell, and finally, the people behind me fell.

A senior gentleman in our group helped me get up. We suddenly heard the call for us to board and hurrying over, the conductor held out his hand for our tickets. Jim realized he must have lost them in the fall.

"What are we going to do? What are we going to do?" I cried, completely overcome by our predicament. At this instant, I looked up and standing between Jim and me was our leader, Betsy Cunningham. Placing her arms around the two of us she said in a most calming tone: "This is no time to panic. It's a time to pray and trust our Father."

She prayed for God's calmness, direction and protection. No sooner had she finished praying than one of our leaders stood, holding both arms high, clutching two train tickets, and saying, "Did someone lose these?"

I had many learning experiences while teaching in China, but none as important for stopping fretting than "This is no time to panic, it's time to pray."

Do not be anxious about anything, but in everything, by prayer and petition, with thanksgiving, present your requests to God. And the peace of God, which transcends all understanding, will guard your hearts and your minds in Christ Jesus.

Philippians 4:6–7

Why Fret Fiery Trials?

SHERYL PATTERSON

Smoke began to billow into my home. Coughing, I made my way to the kitchen where I reached for a dish towel. Pressing it tight to my face, I looked out the window at the raging fire that was engulfing the pined mountainside. Fear and sadness gripped me. The mountains behind the house were so beautiful and full of wildlife. Now death lay upon the land. Would my home be licked up in one quick gulp by this powerful force? All it would take would be a windshift.

Weeks later I hiked the perimeter of this charred, once proud mountain. It looked as if nothing could ever grow there again. But coming down a ravine, wisps of magenta coloring caught my eye. Before me lie single stemmed flowers showing off innumerable blooms of beauty. I was amazed. New life was already taking place.

Visiting the library the next day, I studied and found that this plant was known as Fireweed. It is one of the first plants to grow and bloom after a fire and it seems to enjoy the challenge of growing in adversity. God was able to show me that He can work in any situation no matter how final it may seem.

The gifted composer Beethoven wrote his deepest music after becoming totally deaf. In our journey with God, we also, will have times of hardship and sorrow, but as William A. Ward said, "Adversity causes some men to break; others to break records." Thus, I have decided to stop fretting my trials and instead look at them as opportunities.

When you walk through the fire, you will not be burned; the flames will not set you ablaze.

Isaiah 43:2b

Why Fret "Having"?

MICHELE T. HUEY

"Lord, how can I be content with what I have when what I have is either broken, worn out, or running on a prayer?"

I was in another one of my grumbling moods. Everywhere I looked, it seemed, something needed to be fixed or replaced. My range had one good burner, and the oven could shoot up a hundred degrees in a matter of seconds. The downstairs toilet ran constantly unless shut off by hand, and the temperamental hot water heater practically boiled the water at times. Other times we shivered in cold showers. Both of our vehicles have logged over 100,000 miles and needed repairs. Stuffing oozed out of every pillow in the house, and the dog clawed up my bedspread. *Is this another one of God's lessons in patience for me?* I wondered.

Then during my quiet time reading, I came across a phrase that seemed to jump off the page and address all my complaints: "Being is more important than having." Because I valued *having* before *being*, I was discontented, joyless, and grumpy.

What I needed was a shift in my perspective. I decided, "I will be more content when I purposely look for the good things I still have, not fret about the new things I would like to have."

I still cook on one burner, bake casseroles, and broil chicken. Our vehicles get me where I want to go and are paid for. Even if the showers are cold, I have a warm bed to sleep in, no mortgage, and people who love me. And what's more, I have a Heavenly Father who promises to provide for all of my needs.

I still have problems being content with what I have when something else breaks down. But when I view the tiger lilies my husband and children picked for me and feel a warm tenderness tug at my heart, I know I'm finally beginning to learn.

. . . be content with what you have, because God has said, "Never will I leave you, never will I forsake you."

Hebrews 13:5b

Why Fret Mishaps?

KELLY KING

I sat in the school parking lot. The temperature gauge was climbing and I could tell the van was getting hot. *Just get it home,* I thought. *I'm sure it's nothing.*

Sure, it was nothing. After replacing a radiator fan and spending $600, this little incident became the first in a string of "what's going to happen next" scenarios at our house over the next couple of months.

Two days after the van incident, our lawn mower was stolen from the garage. Two weeks later, the garage door broke. Everyone joked, saying these things usually come in threes. Good. Our three were over.

Little did I know, our "threes" had just begun. The dishwasher broke. Two TVs and a VCR pooped out. And on top of that, our second car was totaled in a wreck on the day of my husband's grandfather's funeral. *God, I know You've promised You won't allow more to happen than what I can handle. But are You through yet?*

In those short months, I adapted to washing dishes by hand (we used a lot of paper plates) and my husband drove his grandfather's '79 Zephyr. Our children had never seen windows you could actually "roll" down without a button. We watched a lot less TV.

Whatever we called them—mishaps, trials or character-building situations (I love that one)—God showed Himself faithful in provision and protection.

First, my husband and father-in-law were able to replace the broken part on the van, saving us a lot of money on labor. Our homeowner's insurance covered the replacement of our lawn mower. No one was hurt in the car wreck and the other motorist's insurance settled on our vehicle in record time. An unexpected financial gift provided a new garage door, dishwasher and new TV.

God is *good*. Better yet, God teaches us *great* lessons. He is maturing us and perfecting us in His timing and in His wisdom. Am I ready for any more "threes . . . or fours . . . or fives . . . ?" I'm not going to fret about it, because I know He'll only give me what I can handle in this power.

Consider it pure joy, my brothers, whenever you face trials of many kinds, because you know that the testing of your faith develops perseverance. Perseverance must finish its work so that you may be mature and complete, not lacking anything.

James 1:2–4

Why Fret Being Type A?

LINDA ROSS DAVIS

"This is your Captain. Our flight time today will be fifty-six minutes at a cruising altitude of 29,000 feet. In a moment, the flight attendants will be serving you. Please sit back, relax, and enjoy your flight."

Being a Type A personality, I always feel the unrelenting need to be productive even during "downtime." So, naturally, I reached under the seat to retrieve my satchel. As I settled in with my work materials, I noticed an occasional "bump" as we proceeded through the clouds. Once the pilot reached cruising altitude, something caught my attention. As I looked out my window, I saw a breathtaking full moon above and dark ominous clouds below. I suddenly felt suspended in space, suspended in time. Surely, we were "floating."

That very instant, I realized I had placed my safety and my life in the hands, minds, and abilities of a flight crew—all fallible human beings. How amazing that I could trust mere humans so completely yet I often have difficulty trusting an omnipotent and omniscient God who always keeps His promises.

Charles Swindoll states that for the Type A individual, one of the greatest challenges will be to completely give the controls to God. In his book, *Laugh Again,* he says: "This is extremely hard for Type A personalities. And if you are the super-responsible, I-can-handle-it individual who tends to be intense and impatient, letting go and letting God take charge will be one of life's most incredible challenges."

This challenge greets me every day. I give my worries to God and say that I'm going to trust Him but I tend to keep fretting about them anyway. *Surely,* I think, *He must need my help.*

I'm determined anew to take God at His Word by consistently making a conscious effort to claim His promise of peace, giving each and every worry to God, and allowing Him to become my focus.

As the saying goes, "Let Go and Let God." Let God's peace guard your heart and mind.

His divine power has given us everything we need for life and godliness through our knowledge of him who called us by his own glory and goodness.

2 Peter 1:3

Why Fret Unhappiness?

RUTH E. MCDANIEL

The woman looked at me with suspicion, which quickly turned to anger as she walked past me. What had I done to offend her? I smiled and said hello!

I was just leaving the grocery store after having a pleasant conversation with the checker, when I ran across one of the most sour-looking people I've ever seen. My natural response was to smile and greet her, which usually elicits a smile in return. But, this time, it back-fired. Instead, she gave me a hateful glare and stomped on by.

Whatever had caused that woman's anger had a good grip on her. Or, rather, she had a strong grip on anger. You see, I believe everyone is free to choose the emotions they sustain, whether it's sorrow, anger, fear, or happiness. Not that you can choose *never* to experience bad emotions—things happen and you have instant reactions to them. But, you can choose whether to stay there, or not. As strange as it seems, some people seem to delight in fretting, self-pity, or sorrow for a time, rather than choose to be happy.

A recent television special on happiness gave research results. Not surprisingly, researchers found that people of faith and those who regularly attend church are happier than unbelievers and non-attendees. One major find astonished them all: people suffering from sickness or poverty are often happier than their rich/healthy counterparts. Why? Because they've turned to God and chosen to be happy rather than miserable.

A young man was interviewed as he sat in his electric wheelchair. Due to a diving accident two years earlier, he was paralyzed from the neck down. What was he doing now? Teaching aliens how to speak English—a career that brought him great joy.

He said, "After the accident, I was bitter at first, but that was too lonely. Then, I discovered the more I gave of myself, the more I got in return, and that makes me happy!"

So, learn from the experts. Choose to be happy, no matter what happens. Give up fretting and ask God to fill you to overflowing with joy and happiness. He will. Then, share it with others—even if they refuse to accept it, like the woman at the store. Pass on your happiness and watch it grow.

. . . the cheerful heart has a continual feast.

Proverbs 15:15

Why Fret Moving Mother?

BARBARA LIGHTHIZER

Only the Lord was going to be able to move my elderly mother out of her home. My brother had been watching out for her, so when he died just before her ninetieth birthday, she was alone. In my mind, it was time for her to move to the West Coast to live with me. I admired mother's independent attitude but now it blocked what I felt would be best. Her pioneer spirit would not give up; she insisted on staying in her home.

Leaving her alone worried me. After several months of fretting, praying, and trying to convince her that she needed to be close to family, I realized that I couldn't force her. Finally, I told the Lord that if she chose to die alone, I knew He would be with her. After giving the situation completely over to the Lord, I found peace.

Several months later, a friend of my mother's called and told me my mother was desperately ill. After mother was feeling better, I gently approached the subject of her moving and this time she agreed.

I wasted no time getting to Denver to interview real estate agents. Due to the age of mother's home and the great need of repair, I knew the house would be on the market for several months. The agent I selected was in the process of writing up the listing agreement when he had to call to his office. An agent in the office overheard the telephone conversation and said he had a client who wanted a home in that area. In less than an hour, my mother's home was sold at top price, in spite of the needed repairs. The timing on all of the many facets of selling a home and moving across the country came together with perfect timing. Within a three month period, the sale closed, I moved her to Portland, sold my townhouse, and bought a home to accommodate both of us.

Now when I begin fretting about family members, I know I can give them to the Lord instead of feeling it is my responsibility to make decisions for them. The Lord will work it out in His time.

He has made everything beautiful in its time. He has also set eternity in the hearts of men; yet they cannot fathom what God has done from beginning to end.

Ecclesiastes 3:11

Why Fret God's Silence?

OSWALD CHAMBERS

Has God trusted you with a silence—a silence that is big with meaning? God's silences are His answers. Think of those days of absolute silence in the home at Bethany! Is there anything analogous to those days in your life? Can God trust you like that, or are you still asking for a visible answer? God will give you the blessings you ask if you will not go any further without them; but His silence is the sign that He is bringing you into a marvellous understanding of Himself. Are you mourning before God because you have not had an audible response? You will find that God has trusted you in the most intimate way possible, with an absolute silence, not of despair, but of pleasure, because He saw that you could stand a bigger revelation. If God has given you a silence, praise Him, He is bringing you into the great run of His purposes. The manifestation of the answer in time is a matter of God's sovereignty. Time is nothing to God. For a while you said—"I asked God to give me bread, and He gave me a stone." He did not, and today you find He gave you the bread of life.

A wonderful thing about God's silence is that the contagion of His stillness gets into you and you become perfectly confident—"I know God has heard me." His silence is the proof that He has. As long as you have the idea that God will bless you in answer to prayer, He will do it, but He will never give you the grace of silence. If Jesus Christ is bringing you into the understanding that prayer is for the glorifying of His Father, He will give you the first sign of His intimacy—silence.

Be still, and know that I am God . . .

Psalm 46:10

(Page 285 *My Utmost for His Highest,* Oswald Chambers, Barbour—through Discover House Publishers, Box 3566, Grand Rapids, MI 49501, 1963. Used by permission.)

Why Fret
Being Remembered?

PEGGY JOAN CUTHBERT

It was difficult for my mother when she came to live with us. She was extremely ill for a while and desperately unhappy about giving up her home and independence. In time, she seemed to grow more satisfied, and although not exactly happy, she was content except for her fear of being put in a "home." I think that fear came from the reputation "old folks" homes had in years gone by. I teased her and said, "As long as you know my name, Mom, you can live here."

We laughed a lot about her forgetfulness. One night, we were celebrating my birthday with the whole family. She was "waxing eloquent" as she was known to do, regarding the day I was born.

She said, "I will never forget the day she was born, and I named her . . ." She paused only slightly and then without concern continued, ". . . whatever it was I named her." Without missing a beat she proceeded as if this was the correct telling of the story. We were all in stitches laughing.

My mother loves me very much, but one of these days she will no longer be able to remember my name. The person I have been able to depend on for moral support, advice and love all my life will no longer be able to help me.

God has told us to bring our problems to Him and let Him handle our stresses and inadequacies. We sometimes forget we have a God who will never forget our names. He knows everything about us and has the power to help us when we're feeling low and inadequate. He has promised that He will never leave us or forsake us. Instead of fretting and stewing, we can call upon Him because He's waiting for us to remember to call on *His* name.

. . . I have summoned you by name; you are mine.

Isaiah 43:1

Why Fret Life's Umbrellas?

PENNY SHOUP

I laugh when I think of my large Quarter Horse mare, Michelle, running from an umbrella, but to her it was a scary monster. I had gone to the corral to put her in because it was starting to rain. Ian, our five-year-old neighbor boy, saw me. He came running from the house with an umbrella. His little legs pumped as fast as they could. When he reached the coral he released the lever and the umbrella flew open. My horse jumped and ran to the far corner. She whirled and ran to the other corner. She kept running from fence to fence searching for a way to get away from the horrible object. Her head held high, her eyes wild, and her nostrils wide, she ran and kicked. We sat on the gate and laughed that she was so frightened of a harmless object.

I straddled the fence and approached her, latching the lead rope onto her halter. Michelle stood trembling, seemingly longing for me to rescue her. She lowered her head, took a deep breath and released it with a *swhish*, causing her nostrils to flutter. Her soft brown eyes looked at me with trust, her whole body relaxing. I had control of her by the rope and she trusted me to save her from the monster.

Just like Michelle, I run from many things in this life that frighten me. As I try to escape in an aimless fashion, I'm sure God in His wisdom thinks I look as ridiculous as my horse running from an umbrella. Yet, God is always there, waiting to comfort me and give me His guidance. I look to him with eyes of trust, fully assured that He is caring for me.

As the eyes of slaves look to the hand of their master, as the eyes of a maid look to the hand of her mistress, so our eyes look to the LORD our God, till he shows us his mercy.

Psalm 123:2

Why Fret The Future?

KRISTEN WELCH

"Kristen, this is Tiffany. She will be your PAL this semester. I'll leave and let you girls get to know each other." I'd just been introduced to a 12-year-old girl who had dirty clothes, tangled hair and hollow eyes. She looked at me and smiled.

I was a senior in high school and involved in a program which offered troubled kids high school pals. As Tiffany began to open up, I learned she'd never met her father, her mother was in prison and she was currently living with her mother's ex-boyfriend. She slept on the floor of a drab apartment and had few belongings.

One day I carried Tiffany's burdens home. "Kristen, what can we do to help her?" my mom asked.

"All her clothes are stained and out of style," I replied. "Could I go through my things?" My mom thought it was a great idea.

The next week, I dragged three huge bags stuffed with everything a preteen girl could want to give to Tiffany. As I saw her hollow eyes shine, I knew we'd done the right thing. I returned the following week to find the school counselor instead of Tiffany. The courts had stepped in and placed her in a foster home in another city. I was not allowed contact. I grieved and prayed for my lost friend.

I graduated that year and moved to college. My senior year in college approached quickly and I fretted about my future plans. I constantly asked God to reveal His plans for me.

I worked at the children's home tutoring struggling students. The director began to introduce my new student, but before she finished her name, Tiffany and I were hugging and crying. At that moment, my world froze as God reminded me, *Kristen, I know where you are. I haven't forgotten you. Trust me. I wanted you to see Tiffany today to remind you to not fret about tomorrow because I hold it.*

It's easy to wonder if God has a plan for each one of us. We fret and question what our future holds. But God holds the future in the gentle palm of His hand. He'll show us step by step.

Therefore do not worry about tomorrow, for tomorrow will worry about itself. Each day has enough trouble of its own.

Matthew 6:34

Why Fret The Sting Of God's Word?

LINDA SHEPHERD

God's Word can be like medicine. But medicine, I've noticed, is often hard to take. At least my young son thinks so. Take the day Jimmy got a scratch on his hand.

Being a smart four-year-old, he knew that I kept the bandages in his sister's Laura's room. Laura, who is brain injured, required constant care and so her nurse greeted Jimmy when he stuck his head in the door.

"Nurse," he lisped, "I need a bandage. I got an owee on my hand."

As the nurse helped him get a bandage out of the drawer, she said, "Let me put a little medicine on your cut for you."

"Okay." Jimmy directed, "But don't put the medicine *under* the bandage, put it on *top* of the bandage."

"But the medicine won't help your cut if I put it on the bandage," Carol said, trying to hide a smile.

Jimmy batted his blond lashes. "But if you put the medicine on my cut, it will sting."

"Well, I think that's the point. The medicine will sting, but it will kill the germs too."

How valid Jimmy's concerns were. Medicine does sting our cuts. Yet as Carol pointed out, it kills germs and it promotes healing.

This is also true with God's Word. When I apply it directly to my situation, it stings. But as God's Word stings me, it also kills the germs of hate, envy, fretting and other dishonorable things. Plus, the power of God's Word promotes healing.

How healthy it is to take a dose of God's Word every day. It may take extra effort, but even when it stings, the results are worth it.

. . . listen closely to my words. Do not let them out of your sight, keep them within your heart; for they are life to those who find them and health to a man's whole body.

Proverbs 4:20–22

Why Fret the Spiritual Fog?

BILLY GRAHAM

Once when I was going through a dark period I prayed long and earnestly, but there was no answer. I felt as though God was indifferent and that I was all alone with my problem. It was what some would call "a dark night of the soul." I wrote my mother about the experience, and I will never forget her reply: "Son, there are many times when God withdraws to test your faith. He wants you to trust Him in the darkness. Now, Son, reach up by faith in the fog and you will find that His hand will be there." Relieved, I knelt by my bed and experienced an overwhelming sense of God's presence. Whether or not we sense and feel the presence of the Holy Spirit or one of the holy angels, by faith we are certain God will never leave us nor forsake us.

The eyes of the LORD are everywhere, keeping watch on the wicked and the good.

Proverbs 15:3

(Page 143, *Hope for the Troubled Heart*, Billy Graham, Word, TX, 1991.)

Why Fret God's Timing?

JAMES DOBSON

In 1945, shortly after the end of the Second World War, a young associate pastor named Cliff and his fiancée, Billie, were anxious to get married, even though they had very little money. They managed to scrape together enough funds for a simple wedding and two train tickets to a city where he had been asked to hold a revival with a friend. By combining this responsibility with their honeymoon, they thought they could make it. They planned to stay at a nearby resort hotel.

The couple got off the train and took a bus to the hotel, only to learn that it had been taken over by the military for use as a rehabilitation center. It was no longer open for guests. There they were, stranded in an unfamiliar city with only a few dollars between them. There was little to do but attempt to hitch a ride on the nearby highway. Soon a car pulled over, and the driver asked them where they wanted to go.

"We don't know," they said, and explained their predicament. The man was sympathetic and said perhaps he could offer a suggestion. A few miles down the road was a grocery store that was owned by a woman he knew. She had a couple of empty rooms upstairs and might be willing to let them stay there inexpensively. They were in no position to be choosy.

The lady rented them a room for five dollars, and they moved in. During their first day in residence, the new bride spent the afternoon practicing the piano, and Cliff played the trombone he had brought with him. The proprietor of the store sat rocking in a chair, listening to the music. When she realized they were Christians, she referred them to a friend, who invited them to spend the rest of their honeymoon in his home. Several days later, the host mentioned that a young evangelist was speaking at a youth rally at a nearby Christian conference center. They were invited to attend.

That night, it so happened that the regular song leader was sick, and Cliff was asked to take charge of the music for the service. What an historic occasion it was! The evangelist turned out to be a very young Rev. Billy Graham. The groom was Cliff Barrows. They met that evening for the first time, and a lifetime partnership was formed. As the Christian world knows so well, Cliff and his wife, Billie, have been members of the Billy Graham Evangelistic Association ever since that evening and have been used by the Lord in thousands of crusades all around the world. I suppose Paul Harvey would say, "And now you know . . . the *rest* of the story."

Isn't it amazing the lengths to which the Lord went to bring these now inseparable team members together? Some would call their meeting a coincidence, but I disagree. I recognize the hand of God when I see it.

Commit to the LORD whatever you do, and your plans will succeed.

Proverbs 16:3

(Dr. James Dobson, pages 135-136, *When God Doesn't Make Sense,* Tyndale, IL. 1993. Used by permission.)

Why Fret
God's Sovereignty?

JILL BRISCOE

Years ago I led a vibrant youth work in the north of England. The young people were mainly unchurched and had lived life without Christ, without God, and without hope. When Stuart and I accepted a call from a church in Wisconsin and began to pack up to leave England and travel to America, I became overly concerned with the welfare of the young people we were leaving behind. While some had matured in Christ, many had only recently come to the faith. If only they would all be mature and grown up in their faith before we had to leave them, I thought. It was a struggle just to think about going. The burden and responsibility weighed me down.

I mentioned this to Stuart, and he simply replied, "You didn't save them—you don't have to keep them!" In other words, it was God's work, not mine! Changing men and women was the work of the Spirit and not dependent upon the doubtful privilege of my constant company. I could safely leave it all in his hands. He had directed me elsewhere.

To realize intellectually that the work we are doing is a God-directed work is one thing; but to do it is another.

In his heart a man plans his course, but the LORD determines his steps.

Proverbs 16:9

(Jill Briscoe, *Running On Empty*, Page 130, Harold Shaw, IL. Revised 1995. Used by permission.)

Why Fret
An Unknown Future?

JANE E. MAXWELL

Drip . . . drip . . . drip the pale yellow liquid filling the clear plastic bag rhythmically slid down the long tubing and pushed through the needle inserted in John's arm. He sat back in the brown recliner with his arm outstretched and resting on a pillow. This was the tenth infusion of these potent miracle drugs. Glancing around, I recognized several other men and women also surrendering their arms to the needles while loved ones or friends sat by their side.

Every since the day the telephone call jolted my mind into accepting the news that Johnnie had late stage cancer and would need massive doses of chemotherapy drugs, I had been fretting and distressed. I read all the literature outlining all the side effects of those drugs, and became even more concerned. However this was my friend's only chance and I had promised him that I would be with him every step of the way.

I had pictured the "chemo room" as a dismal place with sad faces everywhere. What a surprise God had in store for me. We entered a brightly wallpapered room with sounds of music floating through the air. Young and old were swapping tales, sharing jokes and laughing with the nurses. Over the following weeks I saw courage, optimism, and hope written across their faces. Cancer had robbed them of their physical strength and their hair, but they would not let it rob them of their spirit.

Auburn-haired Maryann sat next to us one day. She had been here four years earlier but now her cancer had reoccurred. She was not giving up. She quipped, "Oh, the chemo will make me go bald again but I just tell my husband to buy a can of pledge and keep me shined up."

I laugh with the others. I have learned that I no longer have to fret the God stuff, not now nor in the unknown future. He will always be wherever His children are. As I am able to relinquish my fears and trust in His promises, Johnnie is also at peace knowing God is in full control.

God is our refuge and strength, an ever-present help in trouble.

Psalms 46:1

Why Fret Small Results?

MARILYN KREBS

I had organized a luncheon for the ladies of our church to raise support for a missions project. Announcements were made well in advance. The speaker was prepared. The social hall was artfully decorated. For all that, on the appointed afternoon of the luncheon, only a handful of people appeared.

Frustrated and disappointed, I poured out my complaint before the Lord. After all, I had worked hard to make the event a success. Now, I felt like a failure.

"I'm never going to do anything like that again," I muttered spitefully. "If people are going to be so ungrateful and unappreciative . . . let them get somebody else to try to raise support!"

God calmed my fretting heart. He let me know He was aware of my efforts and that I had done a good thing. However, He chided me about my motives: had I done the good thing for His glory, or to glorify myself? I had to confess my attitude had not been altogether pure and unselfish.

Humbled, I acknowledged that God could take a seemingly unsuccessful effort and turn it into something profitable. He's able to take the smallest offering and feed the multitude. He's *the* expert! Fretting over the God stuff only robbed me of my joy and peace of mind.

To further my lesson on servanthood, God encouraged me to let everything I did for Him in the future, be done with love . . . leaving the results to Him. With renewed vigor I plunged into the next project at hand; deciding that no matter what the outcome, I was going to let God be God.

Always give yourselves fully to the work of the Lord, because you know that your labor in the Lord is not in vain.

Why Fret About A Presentation?

DEBORAH SILLAS NELL

Years ago when I was in college, I was asked to give a short talk at my church on how the Holy Spirit works in our lives. The talk was scheduled for a Wednesday evening. I was honored that I was asked but as Wednesday approached, I began to worry. What would I talk about? I had recently been filled with the Holy Spirit in a dramatic way but knew little about the theological foundation for my experience.

On the Saturday before the talk, I was watering the plants outside the Co-op where I lived near campus. Everyone at the Co-op had a job they performed weekly. Watering the plants was my chore. Fretting deeply about Wednesday night's talk, I paid little attention to the students coming in and out of the building.

One student passed me and said, "So you're the one who makes things grow around here." I nodded and continued to worry about my talk. Another student came along and said, "You're always working." Again I nodded and went back to my fretful thoughts. About this time it slowly dawned on me that these words were attributes of the Holy Spirit. The Spirit *is* always working *and* keeps us growing. *Could this be You talking to me Lord?* The Lord had my attention. What would I hear next?

At that moment another student came along with a tin cup and put it under the water hose. She said not a word. After filling her cup she drank the water and filled it up again. I knew that God was really speaking to me about the Holy Spirit. The Holy Spirit fills us up when our cups are empty and we are thirsty for God's living water.

The Lord had given me my talk for Wednesday night! Even the manner in which God spoke to me was an example of the Holy Spirit working. He is always speaking if we have ears to hear. I never needed to worry about what I was going to say. God had it all planned out.

But the Counselor, the Holy Spirit, whom the Father will send in my name, will teach you all things and will remind you of everything I have said to you.

John 14:26

Why Fret Child Care?

SUSAN KIMMEL WRIGHT

My son was one year old when my maternity leave ran out. Looking at Tony's bright, trusting face, I felt heartbroken, but trapped. My husband was just back to work after two years' unemployment. Now we not only had all our adoption expenses, but another mouth to feed.

"Please, Lord," I prayed, "send the right person to care for my baby. Send someone who will truly love him."

Only a day later, I wondered if my prayers had been answered when an older woman from church took the job. She had her own ideas about child rearing, but I knew she was competent. And it was good that Tony could remain in his own familiar home.

One short month later, though, my vague uneasiness took shape. Our sitter announced she was starting a new job the next day. She felt isolated in our home, surrounded by fields instead of other houses.

I panicked. How could she *do* this to me? Still worse, how could she betray my son?

In desperation, I called another friend from church. Her teenage daughter, who had baby-sat my son occasionally, had just graduated from high school. Could she fill in for a few days?

To my surprise, Marian said she wanted the job permanently.

She was so young that I hesitated, but I knew her training and instincts were good. Most importantly, I knew she loved Tony. "Let's try it."

Within days, I knew it was a match made in heaven. Tony thrived and Marian doted on him, bringing him presents and filling an album with his pictures.

Today, Tony's a teenager and I've been out of the workforce for years. Marian is still part of our lives, as godmother to one of our younger daughters and an adopted family member.

I think back to my agonized, sleepless nights with a sense of shame. I'd seen our bad experience with the first sitter as a mistake, a crisis, never realizing she was part of God's plan. He had only sent her to fill in until Marian graduated, and she'd left when her work was done. When Marian arrived, the pattern of answered prayer became clear. Tony had someone to "truly love him."

When times are good, be happy; but when times are bad, consider: God has made the one as well as the other. Therefore a man cannot discover anything about his future.

Ecclesiastes 7:14

Why Fret Amusement Parks?

SHERYL PATTERSON

Heat waves radiated from the asphalt and a penetrating heat beat down upon me. I pushed on in what is known as a "theme park" or "amusement park." "Amusing" at this point it was not! Children ran around screaming and playing. Where did they get all their energy? With peak crowds and sprawling lines like a giant octopus, I followed the flow of traffic to inflict my body with another series of tortures in what people called an awesome, incredible, "cool" ride. The ride slung you back and forth horizontally, while viciously flipping you upside down before coming to a crashing halt. I believe the challenge was not so much to survive this ride and "tell about it," as it was to keep your lunch down and pray the same for everyone else! A little boy in line ahead of me dropped his ice cream bar on my foot! Running down through my sandal straps, I felt like a large bottle of Elmers Glue. My weariness which had turned to fretting now moved to anger—close to the boiling point!

Life can leave us feeling as if we are on a continual roller coaster. Some days seem filled with busyness, demands and chaos, while at other times, boredom and weariness overtake us as if we're standing in a slow-moving line going nowhere.

How comforting it is to know that Christ at the Cross of Calvary made a way of destiny for us that's neither slow nor boring, and far more exciting than any ride man can invent. God is the inventor of inventions. He invented *you* with love and an incredible destiny designed especially for you.

Now that's more than amusing . . . that's awesome!

I will refresh the weary and satisfy the faint.

Jeremiah 31:25

Why Fret Forgiven Sin?

C. ELLEN WATTS

When my friends John and Shelley began experiencing financial difficulties, John decided to enroll in some night classes in order to better his job situation. All went well until Shelley landed in bed for several days with a bad case of flu. Already struggling to find enough time for the needs of each day, John must now cope with feeding and caring for their four small children before leaving for work each morning.

Stressed from long hours of late night studying and unschooled in the business of serving as substitute Mom, John quickly punished five-year-old Sally when she upset her milk at breakfast.

John's work did not go well that day. During his lunch hour, he fretted about the vivid mental picture of Sally's tear-stained face.

The moment John got home from work, he called Sally to him. Lifting her onto his lap, he said, "I'm sorry. We all spill things. I should not have spanked you for an accident."

Throwing her skinny arms around his neck, Sally hugged her daddy fiercely. Then, leaning back, looking at John with eyes as blue as his own, she said, "Forget it, Dad. That was this morning."

Long after God has forgiven my sin, I sometimes continue to fret over the real or imagined consequences of having transgressed.

In short, I forget that He not only forgives, He forgets. While I'm busy fretting, He has chosen to never recall that my sin happened "this morning."

Love is patient, love is kind . . . it is not easily angered, it keeps no record of wrongs.

I Corinthians 13:4a, 5b

Why Fret
Terrestrial Collisions?

NORA LACIE ABELL

"White-hot asteroid headed for Earth!" screams the headline.

"Where cities stood, there will be only mudflats," one astronomer describes the devastation.

Words like "tsunami," "crater" and "months-long night" scare the daylights out of readers and television viewers. Oh, did we mention this mile-wide hunk of space debris is zipping at us at a rate of more than 17,000 miles per hour?

When scientists from the University of Arizona Spacewatch program announced that Asteroid 1997-XF11 may have a rendezvous with earth on Halloween eve, 2028, the telescopes of the world focused on a bleak part of the heavens, straining to make sense out of the new, frightening data.

Could a collision occur? How close is "too close?" Is this what happened to the dinosaurs? Are we scheduled for an inevitable cosmic collision?

Wait a minute. Aren't we running about fretting "The sky is falling!" like Chicken Little? Let's not forget to execute our God-designed task of reminding a frightened world that, though asteroids, comets, meteors, and other possible horrors hurtle past us daily, God exerts a greater influence on the cosmos. Not so much as a speck of the universe disappears without His authority.

Of course, we need to be vigilant about real dangers, using planetary resources to wisely prepare for disasters. But as we go about the business of paying mortgages, caring for children, and making sure we get to work on time, we need to get on with our calling of faith. We should fear to tread on God's personal property with prognostications, portents of doom, and omens.

Instead, *any* disaster holds marvelous opportunity for Christians! How perfect are God's purposes! Our firm faith in God's precise plan for our planet proves more winsome to the timid and trembling than Hiroshima-sized sermons or terror-teachings. We may gently remind them that the throne is occupied . . . and not by us! There's no reason to fret about the cosmic future!

God, the marvelous Creator and sustainer of life, shines as the real "star" of this upcoming celestial production. The good news that God is mindful of us, that He loves and cares for His creation is not "a near-miss." His gargantuan grace zooms in on this little blue marble with truly titanic impact.

When I consider your heavens, the work of your fingers, the moon and the stars, which you have set in place, what is man that you are mindful of him, the son of man that you care for him?

Psalm 8:3–4

Why Fret
A Home Mission Field?

NELDA JONES

Years ago, God led us into a state-licensed Foster Parent ministry. At one time we had three foster children, besides our four.

I longed to do more for God, but never seemed to have enough time or energy. Our neighbor's three children were also here much of the time, all day and most of the night.

I grumbled and complained, fretted and prayed. I was full of questions, turmoil, and resentment when the neighbor's children would overstay their welcome.

I alternated between resentment and compassion for them, yet I felt there was a reason for them being here, and God convicted me about my resentment.

The children went to church with us occasionally when their mother allowed them to, but I had to do a lot of praying to overcome my attitude.

One day, as I prayed, God spoke to my spirit, and said, "Stop criticizing and complaining and pray for them and their mom."

He assured me that if I would have the right attitude and be obedient to Him, and sensitive to the needs of the children, He would give me the opportunity to teach these children about Him.

As I prayed for forgiveness, the tears overflowed, bringing cleansing to my soul and spirit. Peace, joy and expectation replaced my resentment.

The neighbor's little girl near the age of Tracy, our foster daughter (whom we later adopted) was visiting at the time, and they were playing "school," one of their favorite games.

As I prayed, a child's voice rang out "Story time!" "Teacher" was about to read stories to her "pupil." My heart leapt, and I knew that God was opening the door He had promised me just minutes before. I grabbed a Children's Bible Story book, and soon had their rapt attention as I read them the story of Jesus' birth and sang to them.

I had wanted to witness for God, and sometimes wished I could go to the mission field, but God showed me in an unmistakable way, that I didn't have to go to foreign lands to work in the mission field.

The greatest mission fields are in our own homes, and in our own backyards. But too often when we are blinded by worry, resentment, anger, and fretting, we fail to see the fields which are ripe unto harvest.

. . . I tell you, open your eyes and look at the fields! They are ripe for harvest.

John 4:35b

Why Fret
A Leap Of Faith?

JO HUDDLESTON

One sunny, spring afternoon, my three-year-old granddaughter, Mallory, asked me to push her in the swing. Soon tiring of that activity, she hopped off the swing and scampered up the ladder to the slide. In an instant Mallory discovered that she had a problem: the slide was too hot from the sunshine for her to rest her bare legs against the metal so that she could slide down.

Compounding her dilemma, Mallory didn't know how to re-trace her climb back down the ladder.

I walked toward the slide, thinking that she would ask me to lift her off.

But, without warning, Mallory leapt through the air toward me. In quick reflex, I wrapped my arms around her just as she latched onto me.

Mallory had chosen me as an escape from her perch atop the slide—she hadn't once thought that I wouldn't be strong enough to catch her.

"You catched me!" Mallory shouted, laughing and taking my face in her hands, rewarding me with a kiss. "Momma Jo, I love you," she said, again tightening her arms around my neck.

Mallory's leap of faith reminds me of the simplicity of Jesus' teaching. In His Word, He promises to be with me at my exact moment of need. I am assured that if I accept God's promises with the innocence and the trust of a little child, I can know his peace and not have any need for fretting.

Trust in the LORD forever, for the LORD, the LORD, is the Rock eternal.

Isaiah 26:4

Why Fret Faith?

PATSY CLAIRMONT

It's difficult to be taken seriously when you're 60 inches short. People have a habit of referring to shorties as "cute." "Cute" is what you call a toddler, a house without a future, or the runt of a litter.

One time I was in Washington, and when I was introduced, I grabbed my suit jacket and slid into it as I headed for the stage. I had been speaking for about fifteen minutes when I turned my head to one side and noticed that my left shoulder was four inches higher than my right. Evidently the pad, rather than conforming to the shape of my shoulder, perched on it. Up to that point, I was the only one in the auditorium who hadn't noticed. I was speaking on being dysfunctional and suggested this perched pad was proof of my expertise in the subject.

When I finished speaking, the mistress of ceremonies approached the steps with the back of her dress tucked into her pantyhose. That took a lot of pressure off me.

I wish my height were my only struggle with smallness. Unfortunately, I'm also shortsighted in my faith. I'm one of those "If I can see it, then I can believe it" people.

Zacchaeus was a small man who shimmied up a sycamore tree to give himself a boost. To that extent, I can identify. But his next move made the difference for him in a way lengthened robes or mountainous shoulder pads under his togas never could. He inched out on a limb to glimpse the Savior. He risked the shaky-limb experience of faith and responded to the Lord's invitation not only to come down, but also to grow up.

That day he stepped down from his own efforts to see and be seen and stepped up to the call of the Lord. Zacchaeus still lacked inches, but he gained insight and walked away a giant of a man.

Faith is a believe-it-first proposition, with no promise "I'll get to see it" regardless of how many boxes I climb. That's scary . . . like going out on a limb, huh, Zac?

Now faith is being sure of what we hope for and certain of what we do not see.

Hebrews 11:1

(Pages 29–30, Adapted from *Normal Is Just a Setting on Your Dryer*, Patsy Clairmont, A Focus on the Family book published by Tyndale House, 1993. International copyright secured. Used by permission.)

Why Fret Living For Christ?

LUIS PALAU

In the late 1950s, I read an intriguing book by Dr. V. Raymond Edman called *They Found the Secret*. In it, Dr. Edman tells how highly influential leaders discovered the secret to the Christian life—through the indwelling, resurrected Lord Jesus Christ.

It made no difference if these men and women called themselves evangelists or revivalists; or if they categorized their experience as the "indwelling Christ," the "second blessing," or whatever. All were experiencing the power of Jesus and, as a result, were seeing tremendous fruit.

As I read how these leaders had discovered taking hold of what Jesus had to offer and living it out day after day, it awakened in me a desire to discover that secret as well. Later, when I understood fully that Jesus Christ literally lives in me and that He wants to fill me to all the fullness of God, it completely revolutionized my life and ministry.

The Christ-centered life is not about trying to sweat it out for God. It's not about striving to be faithful or trying to overcome temptation by discipline, Bible study, and prayer. It's futile to fret about pleasing God in our own strength. It can't be *you* doing it. It must be *Christ* within you doing it!

God can hardly wait for us to admit we can't live the Christian life as He intended. Why? Because the only person who could live the Christian life was Jesus Himself, and He is pleased to live in us. We're united with Christ, and He wants to manifest His resurrection life through you and me. That's what the apostle Paul meant when he said, "It's not me, but Christ. He lives in me!"

God wants to show His power in and through each of us, whatever our circumstances and calling in life. That's when we'll stop fretting and start resting.

I have been crucified with Christ and I no longer live, but Christ lives in me.

Galatians 2:20a

Why Fret When God Isn't?

VICKEY BANKS

Before I enthusiastically raced to the hospital to cheer my sister-in-law on during the birth of her first child, I sat down to have my morning devotions. Following my daily Bible reading plan, I turned to Psalm 139—my favorite passage! Tears sprang to my eyes as I once again read that God forms our inward parts and weaves us in our mother's womb.

What a nice passage for God to have me read as I anticipate the birth of my first niece or nephew, I thought. I thanked God for His awesome care in forming him or her, grabbed my car keys and headed to the hospital to see the opening ceremonies of His latest creation!

Potential turned to panic several hours later when the newly-delivered beautiful baby girl couldn't breathe. Our family helplessly looked on as a steady stream of medical personnel scampered to determine what was wrong and what they could do about it. They hooked my new niece, Mandy, up to a ventilator and sent her to another hospital for emergency surgery.

Throughout those first tension-filled days, God continually reminded me of Psalm 139. I realized that Mandy's "problem" had not caught Him unaware. He was not scampering about trying to figure out what to do next. Just knowing that was like having a warm security blanket wrapped around me. I didn't need to fret. Miraculously, Mandy just celebrated her eighth birthday.

I am often amazed at God, but never more than I was on that day. He took a passage He had inspired long ago, in a faraway place, and used it to speak directly to my circumstances. And, He made sure I would see it by putting it in my daily Bible reading plan. Now that's incredible!

God used the beginning days of Mandy's life to remind me of the importance of regularly reading His Word. He used it to deliver me from my own labor pains of fear and worry.

If we're tempted to start fretting, all we need to do is turn to God's Word for a dose of "Fretting Away Solution." He promises to reveal Himself and His plan for our good.

For the word of God is living and active. Sharper than any double-edged sword, it penetrates even to dividing soul and spirit, joints and marrow; it judges the thoughts and attitudes of the heart.

Hebrews 4:12

Why Fret
Finding A House?

PENNY CARLEVATO

We had just two weeks to find a house and move. Our home had sold very quickly and the one we were going to buy had just fallen out of escrow. The interest rates were way up, about 18%! That put a lot of people out of the category of would-be home buyers, including us. I was beginning to fret. What would we do? Our three children kept asking, "Where are we moving to?"

About this same time, our church was honoring our pastor and his wife with a cruise for their 25 years of faithful service. They were looking forward to it, but they weren't looking forward to the party life that exists on so many cruise ships. They were concerned about who their dining partners would be. After spending time in prayer, we all decided the only thing to do about it was to trust God!

So, off they sailed, while we kept up the search for the right house. At the end of the week, they arrived home full of excitement about how God had answered their prayers. Seated at their table was a young, Christian couple on their honeymoon! They all had a great time.

My initial reaction was, *Now, Lord, what about helping us find a house?* It was then that I heard His still, small voice say, "Don't worry about where you will live. If I care enough about who sits at the table with your pastor, I certainly care where you live!"

Peace overwhelmed me. *Yes, He does care about everything.* The very next morning I just "happened" to be the first to arrive at a new rental home on the market. It was just right for us and became our home for a few years.

After experiencing God's provision, my ability to trust Him and refrain from fretting has increased. I still don't trust Him perfectly, but as soon as I start to worry and doubt, I remember His hand upon our pastor and his wife and upon our house. Then I release my cares and know He'll provide for whatever I need.

Then Jesus said to his disciples, "Therefore I tell you, do not worry about your life, what you will eat; or about your body, what you will wear. Life is more than food, and the body more than clothes."

Luke 12:22–23

Why Fret Daily Provisions?

PENNY SHOUP

"Mom, I'm getting cold," five-year-old Stephanie whined.

"I know, honey. I'm trying to get a fire started," I said as I stacked the logs and arranged the kindling the best I knew how. "Dear Lord, please help me start this fire. You know I can never start fires."

A large blaze erupted as the newspapers caught on fire. The true test was several minutes later when the logs started to glow. I breathed a sigh of relief. "Thank you, Lord."

For one winter a fireplace supplemented our heat when the Michigan winter temperature dropped below twenty. I was horrible at starting fires and many times the four children and I got very cold before my husband got home.

In desperation I started to say my prayer before attempting to light the fireplace. It would start! At times, I fretted, wondering if I was asking too often for His help. "Maybe I shouldn't bother Him with such a small request," I thought. But if I didn't, it wouldn't start. I continued to ask Him each time and I was always able to obtain a warm blaze. It turned into a comfortable, easy relationship as I asked Him daily to help me.

One day I was reading the Lord's Prayer and the words, "Give us this day our daily bread," seemed to come alive. It suddenly dawned on me, *When I'm asking God to help me with the fire, I'm doing what He wants me to do! He wants me to come to Him with my every need, even if it seems insignificant compared to the infinite world He controls.*

I realized that if God didn't want us to come to Him with the smallest request on a daily basis He would have said something like, "and give us all the bread we'll need for the rest of our lives." I'm very glad He's interested in our needs each and every day. It certainly prevents me from fretting about praying too much!

Give us today our daily bread.

Matthew 6:11

Why Fret Starting The Computer?

KURT C. WARD

Last spring, my wife and I decided it was time for a new computer. We scoured the ads and researched the models, until we agreed on our choice. With high hopes, we confidently made our purchase.

When we got home, our excitement to set up our system had piqued, and we tore open the boxes. If we could have channeled our enthusiasm and energy into our modem, we would have been the Big Kahunas of Internet surfing.

We laid out the components and cables on the floor of our office. Arranging the packing slips and instructions, we made sure all the pieces were there and all the units were intact. We started with the first task and after 15 minutes of following four pages of instructions, our system was connected and ready to go.

We turned on the power, and much to our surprise, everything worked *as it should*. We were amazed because we actually expected to have to fret about it not working! But why shouldn't it? Didn't we inventory the parts? Hadn't we followed the instructions?

Later that day, I realized I would save myself much fretting and frustration if I followed God's instructions in His Word. I would save myself much angst and anxiety if I would stop and search the Scriptures about whatever it is I'm facing. It's all there: raising the children and running a business; managing a project and mingling with people; withstanding temptation and weathering trials; checking my motives and contemplating my moves.

Just like our computer needs to check its operating system when its turned on each day, I need to boot up with my Bible when programming my character, and processing my choices and my circumstances. I need to be grounded in the Gospel and download Christ's teachings.

And I need to remember God has given me sufficient memory to carry His Word with me wherever I go. It's guaranteed to prevent fretting!

Your word is a lamp unto my feet and a light for my path.

Psalm 119:105

Why Fret
Evil In The World?

MERNA B. SHANK

Reading the *Daily News* is as regularly a part of my morning as breakfast. But that can produce a case of jitters.

When I hear about happenings in the world, I wonder whether it's safe to travel. What if a hijacker boards the plane I do? What if a bomb is in the luggage compartment? Can I trust my next-door neighbor? Am I safe on the street or even in my house?

I need a word from God along with the news. Fear is not His plan.

When I follow His ways, I may not stop criminals, but I can do a lot to keep from being a victim outside of God's will and protection. God reminds me that living in His will is one thing I *can* do.

But Satan retorts, "What about innocent Christians who also have accidents, get sick, or die—maybe as the result of someone else's sin?" Satan would like to have me believe God's Word is not true if a righteous person dies young.

What is God's answer to that? His ways are so much higher than mine, I shouldn't expect to understand everything. God sees the whole world in the light of eternity. I see only my life and only with limited understanding.

If God's mercy allows a wicked man to live here a long time, that's the only happiness he will know; he's but a few years away from eternal destruction. If God allows a righteous man to die young, death for that man is gain. He steps into a glorious existence for all eternity.

Can I live without fear and fretting? Yes, it's possible. God wants me to trust and not be afraid. Trust will believe God is in control even when I don't understand. Trust can be reasonably cautious, yet relax and let God manage what's out of my control anyway. Trust will also rest in God's promises.

. . . but whoever listens to me will live in safety and be at ease, without fear of harm.

Proverbs 1:33

Why Fret God's Guidance?

BEVERLY HAMEL

She was just a little bit of a girl; only seven at the time. I remember that day like it was yesterday. On my way to the bus stop, a little Cambodian girl approached me from across the street. I was going one way, and she, her mother and brothers were walking the other. In a shy manner, she told me that her mother wanted me to teach them English. I didn't know this little girl, but, there she was. Of course, I couldn't refuse her because my heart immediately warmed to her. I was hooked on her courage. Asian girls and women aren't supposed to do anything more than be baby factories. But she and her mom defied ritual and set a new course for themselves and the two brothers.

Later, Sophea told me how scared she was when she approached me as a total stranger. But she did what she was supposed to do—she obeyed her mother. I did what I was supposed to do—see the situation in the light of God's plan. That meeting did eventually change her course in life. She learned God loves her, not because she can make babies, but because she *is* God's baby.

God never does anything without a purpose; nothing is left undone. I didn't intend to teach English-as-a-second-language classes. But God did and He planned it all along. He knew that to get me out of my comfort zone, He would need to begin rocking my little world. Only He realized that in the days that followed, I would hear the true story of the fall of Cambodia from her family. He desired for it to wrench my heart and start a bond that still remains today.

Sophea's courage taught me to have the same courage as I approach God. Because of her courage, her life *and* mine were changed for the better. When I pray to God with the same courage—because He wants to hear from me—my life is changed and so are the lives of those I pray for according to His will.

If you ever fret about God's guidance, just remember Sophea. She obeyed and so can you.

Therefore, brothers, since we have confidence to enter the Most Holy Place by the blood of Jesus . . . let us draw near to God with a sincere heart in full assurance of faith . . .

Hebrews 10:19, 22a

Why Fret "Leaver Right" Burdens?

GLENNA M. CLARK

"Come on, sleepy heads! Hurry up! If you want to learn anything about rock hounding you have to get out to the desert before the sun gets too high!"

As my family began to waken to my brother's hollering and honking in front of our house, I peeked sleepily out our bedroom window. "It's barely dawn, Bud! I didn't know you'd be so early," I protested.

"Okay. So now you know . . . get a move on," he cheerfully called from beside his vehicle. "We'll grab some breakfast in Desert Center. Shake a leg!"

The rest of the family, falling quickly under Bud's jovial spell, were soon spilling off the front porch, all over each other, and wriggling into his van.

"There!" he said. "Now, where's your ol' poky mom?"

I heard his good-natured remark, but I wasn't in any mood to come back with one of my usual retorts. How could I possibly enjoy an outing? Hanging heavy over my heart was the constant reminder of an up-coming ominous lab report.

"C'mon, Sis, sit up here in front with me. What's with the dark cloud? Should we take it along with us or shall we leave it home?"

By mid-morning all of us were scattered across the half-mile section of sand Bud had designated, hunched over and scanning every rock we saw. Squeals of delight filtered through my gloom. Carefree big and little rockhounds raced to peer at each others' rare and "precious" finds. All the while I silently carried my burden. It seemed to weigh me down, like these huge rocks surrounding us. I couldn't get excited. Trying not to dampen anyone's fun I bent over, pretending to be interested in the rocks on the ground instead of the "boulder" burdening my heart.

As we were all piling wearily back into the van to go home, I kicked a rock. It looked different from the others I'd seen and curiosity got the best of me. I picked it up. "Hey, Bud. Look at this one. What kind of stone is it? Is it special? Is it valuable? Maybe it's a real find."

"It's a leaver-right rock." Bud knows a lot about rocks.

"But what's a leaver-right rock?"

"It's a worthless rock, so leave 'er right there," he smiled.

All the way home I pondered the thought of a worthless rock. It seemed to be a word picture for my burden. I was fretting about it when I could just as well "leaver-right" with the Lord where it belonged. The way He said we should.

With the family streaming back into the house, I paused beside Bud's open van window. "Thank you, Bud, for a very special day."

"Glad you left that cloud back there among the rocks, Sis."

Little did he know. Our Lord knew full-well that life has many burdens. He wants to relieve us, but He can't unless we are willing to leave them right with Him.

Come to me, all you who are weary and burdened,
and I will give you rest.

Matthew 11:28

Why Fret Being Unfruitful?

MILDRED WENGER

My husband, Dan, and my daughter-in-law, Bev, have had an on-going competition to see who could raise the first tomatoes. Sometimes Dan even bought his plants in Virginia, hoping they had been started earlier than those from our Pennsylvania greenhouses.

One year Bev added some humor to the game. She came to visit us on a Sunday evening. While the adults talked, her two daughters went for a walk. The next morning Grandpa was surprised to find big, ripe "tomatoes" all over his vines. On closer inspection, he discovered that the girls had tied round red balloons to the stems!

Then 1997 arrived. Dan bought only one tomato plant, but he did everything he could think of to coax it to grow faster. Like Jack's beanstalk, it grew and grew. The foliage was dense and beautiful. "This will be a winner," he said. He was wrong.

Though that huge plant eventually spread out to 9½ x 11 feet, it was absolutely worthless, because *it didn't produce any tomatoes*. We hunted and hunted, but all we could find were a few green lumps—nothing fit to eat.

Often when I looked at that plant, I thought of the fig tree mentioned in Matthew 21. That tree also produced nothing but leaves. Jesus showed his disapproval by causing the entire tree to instantly wither away.

Just as our Lord was disappointed in the fig tree, He is disappointed in us, if we don't bear any "Spirit fruit." It's not enough to say, "Yes, I'm a Christian," or "Sure, my name's on the church roll," and then go do as we please. We have to live in a way that gives credence to our claims.

Galatians 5:22–23 lists the qualities our lives should produce: "But the fruit of the Spirit is love, joy, peace, patience, kindness, goodness, faithfulness, gentleness, and self-control."

This is the "God stuff" that matters a lot. We don't have to fret about being unfruitful because God will be faithful to produce it in us if we stay rooted to Him. But if we don't have those godly characteristics, we are as useless as that gigantic tomato plant. Our Lord is disappointed in us and the world won't believe our witness.

Thus, by their fruit you will recognize them.

Matthew 7:20

Why Fret Having The Door Locked?

GAIL GAYMER MARTIN

My aunt was one of those forgetful people you read about in funny stories. Finding the iron in the refrigerator or the milk sitting in a closet was not uncommon. Once she weighed herself on a scale, holding her shoes in her hand, and another day she accidentally turned the pot roast blue with clothes dye. Life was always one unexpected thing with Aunt Julia.

One day when we stopped by for a visit, she wasn't home as expected, but being a hospitable lady, she left a note on the door: *The key is under the mat.* I'm sure every burglar in town would thank Aunt Julia for her generosity, but her note teaches us a wonderful lesson.

God leaves the key to a relationship with Him under the mat for us every day. We don't need to fear the door to His presence and love will be locked. All he asks is for us to use the key by listening to His Word and trusting in Him. But we aren't very trustful. God tells us faith can move mountains. We read in the Bible that whatever we ask for in prayer, believing, we'll receive. Then what's the problem?

When we try to handle everything ourselves we don't rely on God. We're too busy patching things together when God could make them new again. But that takes faith and trust.

I imagine Aunt Julia found her milk and iron eventually. She didn't worry about the added pound her shoes weighed on the scale. And I know many guests enjoyed her hospitality, even when she wasn't home.

In the same way, God's door is always open, and He's always home for us. When I try to lean on my own solutions, I remember Aunt Julia, and I recall Jesus' words, "Knock and the door will be opened for you."

Some trust in chariots and some in horses, but we trust in the name of the LORD our God.

Psalm 20:7

Why Fret Sorrow?

JANE E. MAXWELL

Three-year-old Jessica knew her great-grandmother well. She had jumped in my car and rode close to me to visit my mother nearly every Sunday for two years. She laughed and hugged Gramma-Gramma as she rode on her lap while I pushed the wheelchair down the long yellow halls of the nursing home. Her "Gramma-Gramma" had suffered a severe stroke, leaving her unable to walk and barely able to talk, but she knew how to show love to this blond-haired sprite and Jessica loved her in return. She delighted in showing her story books, singing songs, eating ice cream with her, and bringing gaily colored flowers in the summer.

Then the day came when Gramma-Gramma's life on this earth was finished. She had closed her eyes for the last time. She had many friends, plus seven children and a large number of relatives who would be attending the funeral. Although I was cautioned against taking Jessica, I felt I had to let her say her last good-bye.

Anxiously, I took her tiny hand and led her up to the casket. How would she react? Was I doing the right thing? I silently prayed.

"Oh, what a beautiful white bed Gramma-Gramma has and she's got all her flowers around her too," Jessica exclaimed. She then looked around for the wheelchair that had always been by her bed and asked where it was. Someone said, "God couldn't carry that way up to heaven so He left it down here."

"Oh, silly," Jessica loudly replied, "Gramma won't need that chair in heaven cause God made her all better and she can walk all over heaven now and even play with the angels." She then went over and kissed her cheek and said, "Bye-bye Gramma-Gramma."

Sorrow turned to joy. Tears changed to smiles. Death was swallowed up in victory as we remembered that in our Father's house are many mansions. He had prepared a beautiful place for Jessica's Gramma-Gramma. I didn't have to fret the God stuff for He had guided a little child to lead us all.

. . . a little child shall lead them.

Isaiah 11:6c

Why Fret Noises In The Night?

JOAN CLAYTON

The March wind was unusually gusty. It was indeed blowing and roaring like a lion. I had to feed "Lady," my husband's horse. She was such a pet and we both loved her. We loved the way she nuzzled us with her soft velvety nose.

Lady saw me drive up and ran to meet me in her lovable, nickering way. I hurried to the barn and poured her feed into the trough. The noise of the wind rattling the tin roof on the barn terrified Lady. As hungry as she was, she would not dare come to her feeding trough. She ran around in circles, nickering nervously. She looked at me pitifully with those large brown eyes.

"Come on, Lady," I coaxed. "It's all right. Haven't I always taken care of you? Don't be afraid. Trust me."

My words echoed in my ears. I had been nervous about Emmitt being away. He had gone to help our son in Oklahoma build a barn. I don't like it when he has to be away. I don't sleep well. I jump at the noises in the night. "He has to be away three more days," I thought to myself, "I think l know how Lady feels."

"Come, Lady," I gently called and held out my hands to her.

Lady came to me, one cautious step at a time. I led her to her feed and she relaxed. She looked at me gratefully and began to eat. She was in her master's care and she trusted me.

Lady had shown me what I needed to do. She stopped fretting. I needed to do that too!

"Forgive me, Lord," I prayed. "Forgive me for being anxious and fearful. I put my total trust in You."

I was able to relax that night and all of the other nights until Emmitt came home. I slept so good! It was all because I refused to fret the God stuff. I, like Lady, had a loving Master, who loves me and cares for me. I am safe in His care because I trust Him. Why do I need to ever fret?

Peace I leave with you; my peace I give you. I do not give to you as the world gives. Do not let your hearts be troubled and do not be afraid.

John 14:27

Why Fret Tough Questions?

KELLY KING

A wise Sunday School teacher told me first grade children ask lots of questions. That couldn't be so bad, could it? Not until my son entered first grade.

The typical after-school interrogation came daily. "Mom, how come the earth goes around the sun?"

In my non-scientific voice, I flatly answered, "That's the way God made it."

"But, Mom, why did He make it that way?"

"I don't know. He just knows what is perfect."

After fifty questions, none for which I have answers, I looked desperately at my inquirer and declared, "Your daily allotment of questions is up. No more questions today."

A curious look emerged out of his frustration and he dared one more. "How do you know how many questions I can ask in one day?"

He has me. He knows there is no "daily allotment" of questions. And he knows there has to be better answers than mine.

As an adult, I still ask questions when I pray. "God, why did my friend's baby die?" "Why are teenagers gunned down at school while they are praying to You?" "God, why is that family struggling financially when they are serving You?"

The wise Sunday School teacher who prepared me for days of questioning children, also prepared me for tackling life's answers. She told parents, "As your children learn to read in first grade, teach them to go to God's Word and find answers to their questions. Teach them to read and understand so that as they grow, they'll know where to find answers to life's tough questions."

I find that advice to be true every day for my children as well as for me. As I go to God's Word, He teaches me more about His character and love. I learn of God's compassion, forgiveness and promises. Best of all, He never tires of my questions. There may not be simple answers to life's tough questions, but God is faithful and He will always give me the answers I need to face life every day.

Ask and it will be given to you; seek and you will find; knock and the door will be opened to you. Which of you, if his son asks for bread, will give him a stone? Or if he asks for a fish, will give him a snake? If you, then, though you are evil, know how to give good gifts to your children, how much more will your Father in heaven give good gifts to those who ask him!

Matthew 7:7,9–11

Why Fret Unfamiliar Places?

FLORENCE FERRIER

My two nieces' visit had been successful and I was taking the girls home. We reached downtown St. Paul at midday and were advancing slowly from one stoplight to another. While Cyndi slept, Diane, who was eight, kept looking at the crowded sidewalks, a very different scene from their quiet home town.

Finally she said, "If I went shopping here, I'd have to hold Mommy's hand the *whole time*!"

The simplicity of her trust in the safety of her mother's hand convicted me of my little faith in my Heavenly Father's hand. Through many diverse, confusing problems, had He ever failed me? In that moment of revelation, I saw my tendency to fret as a failure to use the gift of faith!

A gentle lesson in trusting was scarcely what I expected during that trip. Yet it was exactly what I needed. Even my earthly parents, while they still lived, couldn't help me in every difficult situation. Yet I can hold fast to the Lord's guiding hand throughout any present and future challenges—even as Diane would trust her mother's hand to keep her safe on a crowded sidewalk.

Diane knew the solution for fretting in unfamiliar places, so could I.

The LORD is my light and my salvation—whom shall I fear? The LORD is the stronghold of my life—of whom shall I be afraid?

Psalm 27:1

Why Fret A Broken Spirit?

JAN BRUNETTE

Tears streamed down four-year-old Jennifer's face as her tiny hand tugged at my skirt. "Mommy, Mommy, hurry. The birdie's broken. Help it, please, Mommy."

Picking up my daughter, I held her close in hopes of calming her. "Honey, tell me how it happened. Then we'll look at it together."

"Tommy's cat . . . knocked it out of the tree . . . it's broken, Mommy, it's broken."

With fingers pointing to the large tulip tree in our back yard, we moved to the heartbreaking scene.

Lying on the ground, a young bird fluttered helplessly as one wing appeared deformed. Several bones protruded misshapenly. A number of feathers were missing. In my own heart, I feared for the bird's future. I knew the damage might be too extensive to repair.

"Will it die? I don't want it to die!" sobbed Jennifer.

"I don't know. It looks bad, sweetheart, but we'll put it in a box and take it to the Nature Center. Their loving hands will help in fixing the hurt. Then we need to pray that Jesus will heal the brokenness. Without healing, it will never fly again."

Bowing her head, Jennifer prayed, "Dear Jesus, fix the birdie's wing. Amen."

When the prayer ended, Jennifer smiled with calm assurance. "It'll be O.K. now, Mommy. You'll see. Jesus will fix it."

Recalling the stress and strains of the day, I too felt as if I had a broken wing. I had fretted about it, wondering whether my spirit could be healed. Now I realized Jesus didn't want me to fret even about that, only take it to Him. A tender touch from Jesus would feel so good. I knew what I had to do.

In the solitude of my bedroom, I knelt and prayed, "Dear Jesus, touch my broken wing and heal my spirit. Restore me with Your courage and strength that I may fly again."

In my mind, I heard Jennifer's voice say, "It'll be O.K. now, Mommy. You'll see. Jesus will fix it."

The LORD is close to the brokenhearted and saves those who are crushed in spirit.

Psalm 34:18

Why Fret Embarrassment?

JERI CHRYSONG

I fell flat on my face at my son's baseball game the other day. I was rushing to take a picture of his "at bat," fiddling with my camera, and not paying any attention to where I was going. I went sprawling in front of two sets of bleachers, Home Team and Visitors.

The spectators' sharp, collective intake of breath, punctuated with a smattering of muffled screams, told me my slow-motion journey earthward was grand; it was glorious; it was humiliating. Had I been a spectator myself, instead of the unwilling participate in this life vignette, I would have flashed a perfect "10" score as my fall's execution elicited varying emotions and degrees of awed silence from the crowd, perhaps in appreciation of a truly uninhibited moment.

Sitting in church the next day nursing a badly bruised and scraped knee, I struggled to a standing position with my fellow worshipers to sing something about a panting deer and water. By the time I was able to stand without a grimace, it was time to sit back down so I was unable to sing many refrains of the lovely chorus. However, I did think about the deer, and hinds feet set on high places, and wondered why I've never seen a deer execute a Chevy Chase pratfall.

I don't know much about deer beyond Bambi, yet my impression of these animals is that they live in the here and now, not next week. They don't worry about the meadow being big enough to feed them all, or how they look to other deer, nor do they sit around discussing embarrassing falls and the resultant low self-esteem. Their instincts tell them they are loved and cared for by their Creator, and they act accordingly.

The sermon to which I'd paid scant attention ended and, as I hobbled to my car accompanied by well-wishes for my knee's recovery, I determined to stop fretting on this and past embarrassments. There's nothing I can do about them anyway. To dwell on my embarrassment, other than for a good laugh, would be futile and counterproductive. Besides, even though my feet may stumble, with God's help, I can still reach the high places.

He makes my feet like the feet of a deer; he enables me to stand on the heights.

Psalm 18:33

Why Fret God's Storehouse?

ESTHER M. BAILEY

While my husband and I dined at the home of friends one day, the commotion at the window startled me. The sight of a roadrunner pecking on the window surprised me, but our friends expected the visitor.

"He comes every day and waits to be fed," our host explained. The man went to the door to entertain the bird while his wife defrosted tiny hamburger balls, which she kept on hand for the long-tailed, blue-eyed cuckoo.

Speaking to the bird, the man said, "It's coming. She'll have it ready in a jiffy."

The roadrunner recognized the spoken word; then moved his head to follow the action as his benefactor went from the refrigerator to the microwave. When his meal was served, he quickly gobbled up all the food on the porch, and then ventured into the house to pick up a morsel inside the door.

In learning to trust someone who can supply his need, the roadrunner reminded me that I too have a supplemental source of security. My Heavenly Father has promised to meet my needs from the abundance of heaven's storehouse. To act on my behalf, though, God must first gain my trust.

So far life has not required me to take a giant leap of faith. I have not had to deal with a major health issue or watch my husband or son slip away from me into a coma. Disaster has not destroyed my home or damaged keepsakes of yesterday. I don't have to literally pray for my daily bread.

Nevertheless, a lesson in trust applies to me. If I trust in God, I don't need to fret when reality fails to meet my expectations. After preparing as best I can for the future, I don't need to worry about the unknown. If I have placed my ambitions in God's hands, I need not despair over failed plans.

The more I exercise trust in God for the minor concerns of today, the better prepared I'll be to not fret with any major crisis that may confront me tomorrow. Doctors may diagnose my physical condition as hopeless or financial reverses may render me destitute, but God promises strength to handle whatever comes my way.

You will keep in perfect peace him whose mind is steadfast, because he trusts in you.

Isaiah 26:3

Why Fret Others' Lives?

RUTH GIAGNOCAVO

Almost thirty years have gone by since my brother and his wife decided to divorce. Actually, it was my brother who made the decision, so our sympathies, those of family and friends, lay mostly with his wife, Ann. So also did the feelings of the congregation of the small-town church they attended. They supported her and the two small children, emotionally, spiritually and financially.

As time went by I noticed that Ann had a new hair-do nearly every week. A small spark of resentment spread to my heart. Why should Ann be spending money on such a needless luxury, while practically living off the charity of those who so generously supported her? I worked at a business full time, and I couldn't afford such things. These feelings of righteous indignation began to color my feelings toward Ann.

At that point I called her to ask if she would do some typing for me.

"I'm really busy tomorrow," she said. "I have to bake some bread for my neighbor."

"Oh? You sell home-baked bread?" I asked.

"Well, not usually sell it, but my neighbor is a hair-dresser and she's crazy about home-baked bread. So I bake a few loaves for her every week, and she does my hair in payment."

I don't remember the rest of the conversation because I was left floundering for words and very ashamed of my attitude. It didn't take long for me to realize that I had succumbed to fretting along with envy, resentment and selfishness. Additionally, I had spread gossip about her. I had judged her wrongly. I was truly sorry and asked God for His forgiveness.

I learned a valuable lesson that day. God and *only* God can be a judge. He alone knows our hearts and doesn't need us to fret what only He's responsible for. We may think we see the motives and intentions of others, but only He knows everything about someone. If we're pointing at others, we won't notice the three other fingers pointing back at us.

Do not judge or you too will be judged. For in the same way you judge others, you will be judged, and with the measure you use, it will be measured to you.

Matthew 7:1–2

Why Fret
Not Having Hope?

ROBERT H. SCHULLER

I have seen families in this church that have withstood experiences that would crush others. One of these families was the Van Allen family. Both Ed and Jeanne are now gone, having passed away much too young. Ed Van Allen died when he was transporting a new airplane to a South Pacific mission station. The plane never made Honolulu. No sooner did Ed die than Jeanne got cancer. Jeanne was told that her case was terminal, that she did not have long to live. After courageously fighting a losing battle, she suddenly had a last resurgence. She came back and did some wonderful work and made some fine contributions.

At her deathbed, I asked, "Jeanne, where did you get the power to come back these last few weeks? Three months ago you were almost dead."

She said, "Oh, I began to think, 'This is it. You're terminal. Now's the time to quit, give up.' But then I prayed and this thought came to me: If I give up, two organizations will benefit—the mortuary and the cemetery. But if I hang in there for another month or so, my family will benefit. Maybe my church can benefit.

"So I said to myself, I'm going to get dressed at least once more, and I'm going to work on the telephone—the NEW HOPE Telephone Counseling—at least one day, or at least a couple of hours."

She said, "Then I began to get inspired. I thought of hundreds of things I wanted to do. I just kept saying, 'I'm gonna do this, I'm gonna to do that.' Dr. Schuller, the *'gonnas' got me going!*"

Jeanne didn't give in to the flattening-out experiences.

But thanks be to God, who always leads us in triumphal procession in Christ and through us spreads everywhere the fragrance of the knowledge of him.

2 Corinthians 2:14

(Pages 107–108, *Tough Times Never Last, But Tough People Do!* Robert H. Schuller, Crystal Cathedral Ministries, 1983. Used by permission.)

Why Fret Perfectionism?

LYNN MORRISSEY

As a professional church soloist, I strive for accurate intonation and pronunciation, good breath control and projection, sensitive interpretation, and such familiarity with the score that I can sing nearly from memory. But until one life-changing experience, I always thought I fell extremely short of my aspirations.

One Sunday, all professional decorum melted as my high C collided with the organ's piercing C-sharp. Though it was my error, mid-song I had no recourse but to sustain the glaring wrong note.

After the service, a beautiful, radiant woman named Grace, lavished me with undeserved praise. Embarrassed by her compliments, eyes downcast, I lamented, "But Grace, didn't you hear that awful note I caterwauled?" Without hesitation, she encouraged, "Lynn, how many right notes did you sing?"

I was dumbfounded. How many right notes had I sung? Hundreds? Thousands? Hundreds of thousands?

Not just in that song, but in all those preceding. And how many would I sing in those to follow? With God's grace and enabling, my right notes far surpassed the wrong, but I'd never noticed them.

I suddenly realized that while God requires I confess my sins, to constantly fret over perfection, berating God-given talents is sin, as well. My self-flagellation masked underlying sins of ingratitude and unbelief.

My negativism also flowed freely to others. My ears were insensitively tuned to hear only their wrong notes. How many right notes had people sung? How many resounding chords, lilting descants, and graceful arpeggios? My ears plugged by criticism, I missed exquisite oratorios of right notes. And family and friends had missed much-deserved praise—my "well done's" and bravos for their glowing accomplishments.

My one wrong note sung so many Sundays ago, literally changed my life because it fell on Grace's discriminating ears—ears deaf to mistakes and open to achievements.

No matter how many wrong notes I continue to sing (and I do), I won't allow them to drown out my praises to God for all He has given me. And may I never cease to sing the praises of all God's people. Now when they sing wrong notes (and they do), I stop to ask, "How many right notes have they sung?" The wrong ones simply pale by comparison.

But encourage one another daily.

Hebrews 3:13a

Why Fret The Past?

ELLEN BERGH

Here's a little piece of wood, an inch long. If I asked you to carry it for me, it would be easy to put it in your pocket and forget about it.

But if I handed you a ruler, would you forget about it? Within a few minutes, it would annoy you in your pocket.

Would you carry a yardstick for me? Of course not! It won't fit in your purse.

Yet, how often we fret under a much larger load as we carry the past in our mental pocket. We try to walk normally, but instead, we're distracted and fretting, obsessing about something from yesterday. How can we hope to live *today* effectively with such a distracting load?

God gave us the gift of memory to savor the past, not to beat ourselves up about it. If we have asked and accepted His forgiveness, He has no record of that event we're using against ourselves. We aren't designed to carry the crushing load of yesterday or fret about what tomorrow will bring. Carrying that yardstick from yesteryear can make our shoulders droop and our backs ache.

When our thinking gets snagged on the splinters of the past, it's time to turn to the Master Carpenter to smooth away the hurt. He tells us to live one day at a time.

When life overwhelms me, I can stop and ask, "What ruler labeled 'worry' am I carrying in my mental pocket? What yardstick of a past event is bulging from my purse? Lord, I'm taking them out right now and putting them on your Carpenter's bench. They belong to You."

My pocket is empty! I'm free to walk without worrying or fretting. What a relief!

What are you carrying in your pocket?

Take my yoke upon you and learn from me, for I am gentle and humble in heart, and you will find rest for your souls. For my yoke is easy and my burden is light.

Matthew 11:29–30

Why Fret Old Sins?

JO HUDDLESTON

Scrapbooks usually contain no tokens of bad memories; we save only good mementos. In a thick book with sturdy blank pages, we collect a lifetime of pleasant keepsakes. Later, we'll drag out the old scrapbook and delightfully relive our good times through its pages.

Sometimes, however, when we mentally review our life, we dwell on regret and self-reproach. In our mind we've filled volumes with past sins. Our mind's eye recalls the ugly grievances we try in vain to forget: rebellion, disobedience, and our lack of praise and thanksgiving toward Him. If we have repented and been forgiven for these and other sins, we create our own guilt when we choose to remember them. That's fuel for fretting.

But we don't have to fret about past sins because God says that when He forgives us, He also forgets our sin. He separates us from our sin as far as the east is from the west. Why can't we be as kind toward ourselves?

We build scrapbooks like God treats sin: only good memories are retained. With God's help we can stop fretting old sins. We can release our forgiven sins, and then forget them. God has.

I will forgive their wickedness and will remember their sins no more.

Hebrews 8:12

Why Fret Unwanted Pounds?

KRISTIN HUNTLEY

I stood in front of my closet hoping for a fashion miracle. Two pregnancies in two years had left me in need of one. My little darlings had left a few things behind on the way out, namely, unwanted pounds around my middle and stretch marks in places even my pregnancy books never imagined. I had fifteen minutes to find something to wear to church; the only event of the week where my "mom uniform" (old sweats and a T-shirt) would be inappropriate.

In the past weeks after giving birth to my son, I was becoming increasingly fretful about the process of getting back into shape. Daily exercise and a sensible diet weren't bringing results I could see right now. My closet full of too-tight clothes hung there mocking me. I was ready to give up and head for the nearest Dairy Queen.

Have you ever felt like change was slow to come? You've focused appropriate attention on a troublesome area in your life only to be frustrated by setbacks and slow progress? Pouring over one of my many fitness manuals later that day, I stumbled across a formula which spoke to the frustration I felt. Power = strength over time.

I gave that some thought. Maybe my clothes were too tight today, but I was doing the right things. I would be back to my old self, or at least a facsimile of the former me, in no time.

As the formula echoed in my mind I began to see its application in the area of my relationship with the Lord. Many times I struggle with a particular sin, and commit to overcoming it through prayer and Bible study, only to find myself on my knees confessing it all over again. It seems I'm getting nowhere. But, over time, I slowly emerge victorious in the Lord's power. What once consumed so much of my energy is no longer a struggle. With God's help I grew in power.

I needed to be reminded I would be victorious if I didn't give in to discouragement and fear about getting back into shape. I guess I'll have to throw out fretting along with the Ben & Jerry's.

But we are not of those who shrink back and are destroyed, but of those who believe and are saved.
Hebrews 10:39

Why Fret Lack Of Control?

LIZ CURTIS HIGGS

Most of the time I live like an overwhelmer rather than an over-comer. With a too busy schedule and too many demands that I can't seem to say no to, I run around like the proverbial headless chicken, about to collapse. It's a sure thing that when my stress builds up, I get in big trouble.

One afternoon, with a plane to catch and too much left to do, I tore into the house through the kitchen and promptly knocked over the cat's milk dish. I don't mean I bumped it, I mean I launched it with my toe and milk went all over my freshly mopped floor—in fact, the cleaning lady was pulling out of the driveway even as it was happening.

Furthermore, I now had warm milk all over my nice new shoes. Not water, which might dry unnoticed. Milk.

Needless to say, I was not happy, blessed, or feeling like an over-comer. This was not the first time I'd knocked over the cat dish, just the worst time. At the top of my lungs (after all, it was midday and the house was empty), I shouted, "That ?@#$%%! will have to go somewhere else!"

At that exact moment, the door to our downstairs bathroom

began to swing open, and the face of our house painter appeared, wide-eyed and fear-stricken.

Beet red, I stammered, "Oh! No, no, not you! *You* are welcome to go . . . anywhere you like. I was talking to the cat dish."

The what?

"Sure, ma'am," he said, sliding past me as he bolted for the back door and certain safety.

I slumped into a chair, embarrassed and laughing at my foolishness, yet deeply ashamed by my lack of control. *Why can't I overcome, Lord? Why do I succumb to old habits? Why don't I "Let go and let God," instead of letting 'er rip?*

Oh, wretched woman that I certainly am. Who will get me out of this mess? The Overcomer: my Lord and Savior who forgives me when I fail yet persuades me to press on for higher ground and be an over-comer like him.

PS. I tracked down the painter and asked his forgiveness too!

. . . for everyone born of God overcomes the world.
This is the victory that has overcome the world,
even our faith.

1 John 5:4

(Pages 74–75 *Mirror, Mirror on the Wall, Have I Got News for You*! By Liz Curtis Higgs, Thomas Nelson, TN, 1997. Used by permission.)

Why Fret Mistakes?

DORIS SCHUCHARD

"I-R-R-E-L-E-V-A-N-T," Matt paused between each letter, fingering the tiny cross in his pocket. He peered cautiously at the judge, waiting for the buzzer to ring out a misspelled word, but the judge just smiled. Matt had won the school spelling bee.

Flashing a grin of relief, Matt accepted the high-fives and poundings on his back as his classmates crowded around...until Ashley stepped forward. "Well, at least you didn't miss 'pretzel' like last year," she teased.

Matt walked back to the classroom with his friends, but now his shoulders slumped a little lower, his smile faded slightly.

Mistakes. Years from now will Matt remember the many words he spelled correctly? Most likely he will focus on the one word that brought him down.

How do we view our past? If you're like me, I tend not to concentrate on the positive ones like the times I stayed up late to finish a Halloween costume, sat through a little league double-header in 90 degree heat, and read favorite bedtime stories night after night.

Instead, it's the mental tapes of negative events that are replayed, like when I shook my son for dumping out every needle and spool of thread in my sewing box. I remember his shamed silence as I entered the room, the colors of thread strewn about, and the bewildered look on his face. But most of all, the horrible feeling in my stomach when I realized what I'd done.

What's really important is not the error but the attitude about my error. When I see my mistakes as a failure, I believe I'm not up to the challenge, whether it's the challenge of parenting, career, relationships or life. But when I choose to learn from my mistakes I am *going on* instead of *giving up*.

God doesn't fret over my mistakes, in fact, He doesn't even remember them after I confess them. He "blots out my transgressions and remembers my sins no more" (Isaiah 43:25). If God is in the business of forgetting, so should I. I can use my mistakes as an opportunity for growth, discovering what went wrong and asking forgiveness. Allowing God's power to change my circumstances and empower me to try again, I will leave my mistakes where they belong—in the past.

Forget the former things; do not dwell on the past. See, I am doing a new thing!

Isaiah 43:18–19a

Why Fret
Sowing Spiritual Seeds?

DONELLA DAVIS

It was the last day of school. Students had gone home and I was organizing my eighth grade classroom before I left for the summer. Suddenly, a cheerful voice behind me said, "Hi, Mrs. Davis." I turned around to see Brad, one of my students from the year before. After we talked for awhile, I felt a clear prodding from the Holy Spirit to witness to him.

I prayed a quick prayer for God's wisdom and asked, "What are you doing this summer?"

He became solemn as he said, "Watch TV and be totally bored."

"Really? My summers are always filled with church camps and teen trips. Why don't you find a church teen group and get involved?"

Quietly, he replied, "You don't know my background. God could never love me."

I did know some of his background. Brad had been forced to shoot his stepfather out of self defense a couple of years before. I tried to convince Brad God loved even him. The subject was changed and then he left.

For a year, I apologized to God for not leading Brad down the "Roman road to salvation." I felt like a failure as a witness. Surely, God was disappointed in me.

The next year on the last day of school I again saw Brad.

"Mrs. Davis," he excitedly said, coming toward me. "I did what you suggested. I went to church camp and on teen trips. And, Mrs. Davis, I gave my heart to Jesus last summer and I've never been happier! I want to live my whole life for Jesus!"

Lesson learned, Lord! I had been so frustrated with my Christian witness that I failed to realize that the Holy Spirit's prodding that day in my classroom was to plant a few seeds. I should have trusted God to reap the harvest in Brad's life.

Sometimes God needs us to be the sower and sometimes the reaper. We only need to be concerned about obeying, not the harvest. If we keep that perspective, we won't fret about our witnessing.

Even now the reaper draws his wages, even now he harvests the crop for eternal life, so that the sower and the reaper may be glad together. Thus the saying 'One sows and another reaps' is true.

John 4:36–37

Why Fret Feeling Insignificant?

EUNICE ANN BADGLEY

I feel so insignificant. I have not traveled extensively. I am not a career person. I was a stay-at-home mom. I often feel lonely and find myself fretting over things I have not done.

Perhaps it's for these reasons that I find it interesting to focus on people in the Bible that seem to be insignificant.

The innkeeper played a role in the Christmas story. He gave Mary and Joseph the best that he had to offer, even though it was only a stable. But we don't even know his name.

The young boy who had the fish and loaves that fed the multitude was there among the crowd. We don't know his name either, but Jesus used his small lunch to perform a miracle.

The widow who gave her two coins as an offering to God also remains nameless to us but her gift was important.

We are all important to God. He knows each of us by name and we are significant in His eyes. After all, He gave us His Son. If I'm that valuable to Him, then I don't need to fret feeling insignificant.

For God so loved the world that He gave his one
and only Son.

John 3:16a

Why Fret Broken Ceramics?

MARIE ASNER

My young niece was visiting me one day. Though forbidden to touch my collection of small china dogs, she held one and accidentally dropped it. It shattered. She looked up at me and said, "Aunt Marie, make it well again."

I tried to glue the pieces together, but to no avail. There were gaps and holes and the poor china dog looked like a composite of dog and cat when I was finished.

I told her that "making it well" sometimes means it won't look the same but will be a new creation, functioning with a new purpose. My instruction also included, "Don't touch Aunt Marie's china dogs without permission."

As we travel through life, we encounter situations that break us whether we have done something carelessly or don't know if we have done anything wrong. They just happen. For example, we may have parked in a handicapped area when the parking lot paint was so faded we didn't know it was a special area. Or maybe we moved ahead of someone in the grocery line while we were engrossed in the latest tabloid magazine. We annoy someone without realizing what we have done.

God is never annoyed with us. Though we may feel "broken"

over an incident, turning the experience over to God will "make it well" though we may not be the same again.

Have you received a warning for parking in a handicapped zone? Become an advocate of disability rights. Have you been confronted with errant behavior at the supermarket? Smile and move aside.

Don't fret about mistakes. Just correct it the best you can and go on.

. . . turn to God, so that your sins may be wiped out, that times of refreshing may come from the Lord.

Acts 3:19b

Why Fret God's Purposes?

ESTHER M. BAILEY

During his sermon on Elijah, the pastor made a profound statement: "Sometimes the most spiritual thing you can do is take a nap." I like that brand of theology.

After witnessing one of God's greatest miracles, Elijah sat under a tree in the desert fretting about Jezebel's threat to kill him. Considering himself to be a failure, the distraught prophet asked God to take his life. God's prescription: food, water, and sleep to provide strength for his designated journey.

Sometimes I see myself in Elijah's behavior. No one is trying to kill me, but I get discouraged when my efforts in ministry fail. An editor may reject an article I believed to be inspired by the Holy Spirit. With my soul invested in a project that contributes nothing to God's kingdom, I feel like quitting.

At other times failure spurs me on. I vow to think deeper and work harder, often in my own strength. My ambition exhausts me and robs me of creative ideas.

Life's interruptions also frustrate my efforts to accomplish something I believe is God's purpose. After two or three days away from my computer I begin to fret.

I can't get back on track until I turn to God for help. I pray for rest for my body and mind. When a good night's sleep renews my spirit, I ask God for Holy-Spirit-inspired ideas. If I keep myself out of the way and let God work, results are much better.

Oh yes, I continue to send out the article that caused me so much pain when rejected. Somewhere along the line, maybe on the twelfth try, the article is accepted. The article may even be published in a magazine with a greater circulation than where I originally sent it. Or the readership may be far less. Whether I have a million or a thousand potential readers I pray that the article will reach someone who needs the message.

Why doesn't God direct me to send the article to the right source in the first place? I don't know and I'm going to quit wondering. After all, that's God's department. Fretting doesn't give greater insights.

. . . when you lie down, you will not be afraid; when you lie down, your sleep will be sweet.

Proverbs 3:24

Why Fret Unexpected Expenses?

COLLEEN GUERRETTE

It was financial calamity with a vengeance. It started out, appropriately enough, on Monday. While driving on the freeway, an ominous "zzzt" sound coming from somewhere under the dash caught my attention. Probably a fuse, I reasoned. Nothing serious. That "zzzt" translated into $239.00 in electrical repairs. (Bummer!)

On Tuesday, our tax accountant tallied up an extra $366.00 we were found to owe the state of California. (Ouch!)

On Thursday, a smiling, polite police officer pulled me over and wrote me a traffic citation. The fine plus traffic school exceeded a whooping $500.00 (Groan!)

All these unexpected expenses! What was I to do? My brain was muddled with questions: *How are we going to pay for all of this? What did we do wrong? Is God testing us?*

As usual, my husband, Andy, the stable one who never frets about anything had some sage advice: "Don't worry."

Don't worry? Oh sure. Being the money manager in our house, I had to worry, now didn't I? If I didn't worry, who would? If I didn't sweat and fret, shout and pout, cry and sigh, mumble and grumble, who would?

Sensing my consternation, Andy took my hand and led me to sit down on the couch. "Has God ever let us down?"

"Well . . . no," I answered.

"Do you think this little $1,200 challenge is too big for God to handle?"

"Well . . . no."

"Do you think God was lying when He said He would supply all our needs according to His riches in glory in Christ Jesus?"

"Well . . . no."

I had to admit, his questions were a lot better than mine. It's a good thing one of us has a cool head. We prayed and I repented of my lack of faith.

The next afternoon there were two unexpected checks in the mail: a refund from an overpayment and a forgotten expense check that Andy had turned in months ago which for some reason had been delayed until this moment. Not only that, but when Andy came home that night, his paycheck reflected a raise retroactive six months.

Well, wonder of wonders, all this extra, unexpected money was exactly enough to cover those extra, unexpected expenses. Every one of them.

You and I never have to fret about finances because God knows the need and has more than enough resources to take care of it. As we show our faith in Him, He'll respond with abundance!

Great is our Lord and mighty in power; his understanding has no limit.

Psalm 147:5

Why Fret A Beef Roast?

GAYLE CLOUD

Several years ago our family was in a place of great need. My husband was out of work. We had gone without any income for over six weeks. Our bills were piling up. Even worse, with two young children, our laundry was piling up—and I was totally out of detergent! We had prayed and waited and waited. We fasted and prayed. We had no direction and we began to fret about God's ability to provide.

We finally received an anonymous monetary gift. Then we had to decide which bills should be paid. Our first decision was to tithe. That was a tough one! We had so many bills and so little money; yet we knew we had to take a step of faith. We felt prompted to give a bit differently than usual.

Good friends were struggling nearly as much as we were, and we decided to take the money and buy some groceries for them. The Lord had always provided sustenance for both of our families, most especially in the form of vegetables, beans and bread—the basics. We decided to buy some fun food for our friends in need. We bought some ice cream, potato chips, some necessities—and a beef roast. Oh, that roast was beautiful. I longed to be able to buy such a roast for my own family, yet I was excited that we could buy such a roast for our friends.

After our shopping trip was completed, we took the groceries to our friends, rejoiced in the goodness of the Lord and returned home. No sooner had we walked in the door, than some friends entered our house with three bags of groceries. While the bags contained no ice cream and snacks, they did contain a wonderful, large beef roast. We could not believe our eyes! No one knew how we had longed for that roast—except God. Not only did this event increase our faith, it became a marker of God's faithfulness to our family. Whenever we are tempted to fret about God's goodness today, we review our family history and see not only a very caring God, but One who has a great sense of timing!

. . . but to put their hope in God, who richly provides us with everything for our enjoyment.

1 Timothy 6:17b

Why Fret Giving?

CHARLES STANLEY

We were receiving money one Sunday in 1980 toward our new church property, and people were coming forward to give all kinds of things—cars, houses, property. A woman walked forward and took off a large gold bracelet and put it in my hand. She said to me, "This is the most valuable thing I own." (The bracelet was, indeed, valuable. It sold for $17,000 when we turned it in for the church building fund.)

When the woman dropped that gold bracelet into my hand, however, the Lord spoke in my heart and said, *You've never given Me anything but money.*

My thoughts turned immediately to my cameras. Now, I love to take photographs. That's my hobby. Down through the years, I had acquired quite a bit of camera gear. And I thought, *Oh, no, Lord, that's asking too much.* But I knew instantly that selling my cameras was what I had to do.

The next day, I got all my camera equipment together and took it down to a friend who bought and sold used camera equipment.

I had felt strongly impressed that we were to give at least $5,000 more than we had given. I had saved about $1,600. The camera store owner went into the back and figured up what he could give me on my cameras, and he came back and said, "How does $3,420 sound?" I said, "That's perfect."

I gave the $5,000 the next service. I had given my cameras, but emotionally, I was still holding on to them. The day came when the Lord reminded me of the verse in the Bible that says, "Where your treasure is, there your heart will be also" (Matthew 6:21). I decided that I would choose, by my will, to link my heart to what God was doing in our midst rather than to a collection of shutters and lenses and film holders.

In that moment, I truly gave those cameras to the Lord.

Several months later, a woman rang the doorbell of my house. When I answered the door, she said, "Are you Charles Stanley?"

I said, "Yes, ma'am."

She said, "Here!" and she handed me a suitcase and a paper bag.

I brought the suitcase and paper bag inside, and I found in them every single item of the camera gear that I had sold and given to the Lord. Every camera body, every lens, and every filter was there.

I've had a *triple* joy from that experience of giving my cameras. The single joy was the genuine joy of giving those cameras to the Lord—of truly giving them out of my heart as sacrificial giving of treasure to the house of God. That joy would have stayed with me all my life, even if I had never seen those cameras again. But that isn't the way God works. The Lord could have chosen to give me back anything He wanted. He had no obligation to give me back those cameras. And yet, that was His pleasure, and I had the double joy of receiving back my camera gear.

Remember this: Whoever sows sparingly will also reap sparingly, and whoever sows generously will also reap generously.

2 Corinthians 9:6

(Charles Stanley, pages 169–171, adapted from *The Source of My Strength*, Thomas Nelson, 1994. Used by permission.)

Why Fret Mental Battles?

SUZANNE J. GRENIER

While chatting with my oldest sister in her refurbished kitchen, our conversation drifted into monetary matters. She exuberantly asked, "Guess how much money I have in my thrift account?" My shoulders shrugged. Without hesitation she responded, "$52,000."

I was glad for her. She married at 20, raised two daughters, then started college in her late 30's. As icing on the diploma, she also had a 3.94 cum. In spite of my happiness for her, irritating thoughts crept in. *She's making about $20,000 more than I am. She's been working for only eight years. I've been working for 25! It's not fair! Before I attended Bible school I was making about $10, 000 more than I am now. That was seven years ago! I should be making more money!*

It was true. In 1991, I left an employer I had worked with for thirteen years and decided to attend a one-year Bible school. After graduating, my plans of working for a Christian organization or a church didn't line up with God's. Thus, under sovereign guidance, I reentered the so-called more "secular" work force. In six years I've held four administrative assistant positions, ranging from $10,000-18,000 less than my previous income.

Then another inner voice gently interrupted: *You know money isn't that important. You also know you can't let it rule your life.*

As in times past, I could have allowed this scenario to continue to throttle my contentment. Yet I decided to cool the engine of swirling thoughts with a "quick spirit check." Which thoughts were God's and which were Satan's? Which set of thoughts lined up with the Word of God? The first set conveyed jealousy. That wasn't God. The second set reminded me of these Scriptures: "The love of money is the root of all kinds of evil." "You shall have no other gods before me." That was God.

Now it was Satan's turn to fret about that God stuff. Since Jesus combated Satan with His sword, the Word of God, I followed Him in suit. I unsheathed my spiritual sword and wielded, "Get behind Jesus, Satan!" Naturally, Satan had to flee.

Ah, sweet peace returned!

Now whenever any mental discourses occur, I do another "quick spirit check" with a sword in hand. It saves fretting about mental battles.

Wisdom is a shelter as money is a shelter, but the advantage of knowledge is this: that wisdom preserves the life of its possessor.

Ecclesiastes 7:12

Why Fret
The Pumpkin Patch?

MARILYN NEUBER LARSON

I became Pumpkin Queen a couple of years ago when I relinquished my status as city-slicker, retired from teaching school, married my farmer-hero, moved to the country, and adapted to Jake the Snake who lives at the back door.

Bill, my new husband and pumpkin farmer, worked harder than a team of draft horses, but pressing expenses strained our finances tighter than last year's jeans.

If you'd asked me a few years ago what a crop cost, I'd have guessed some seed, a little manure, and bug spray. I had no idea it resembled the national debt, which keeps us in chronic arrears.

I prayed for provision, and prayed about trusting, and fretted about fretting. One day God showed me my money worries damaged my relationship with Him. I should approach Him like a child, asking Him to provide, but then I needed to believe that He would answer.

During harvest, phones ring incessantly as Bill markets the crop and sends semi-loads of pumpkins down the road. When we married, I'd envisioned romantic candlelight dinners, but settled for supper at the truck-stop.

One Friday it rained torrents at our pumpkin funny farm, with muddy roads holding seven eighteen-wheelers hostage at the truck stop. Workers wearing rain-slickers cut, loaded, and slid in slimy-slick fields harvesting pumpkins. At quitting time the yellow slickers lined up at our door.

The check that was supposed to be in the mail hadn't arrived, and it was time to pay our workers. In the bedroom Bill emptied his wallet and I dumped my purse, but we were still $60 short.

"Lord," we prayed, "show us what to do."

In that instant He reminded me, "Look on the top shelf in that zippered bank bag."

With shaking fingers I pulled the bag from its hiding place and counted out exactly $60, a long forgotten overdue deposit.

I stood frozen in awesome thankfulness. How could I continue to fret and doubt God's goodness? Jehovah Jireh, my Provider, had proved that when we ask—and believe—He not only answers, He gives us peace.

This is the way he governs the nations and provides food in abundance.

Job 36:31

Why Fret Paying Bills?

MERNA B. SHANK

I needed more than a thousand dollars by Wednesday. My husband who managed our family business and my daughter who did the bookkeeping were both away for several weeks, so I was especially busy with my own duties plus some of their work. When I realized that payroll taxes were due on Wednesday, I didn't know where I would get a thousand dollars, but I prayed.

Praying for funds was not new to us in the twenty-five years we had operated our printing business, but times had become easier after several years of growing pains. Now, however, funds were shorter again as we carried some accounts longer than thirty days to help another Christian business through its fledgling years.

Monday's work included reconciling the latest bank statement so I would know for certain that my records were accurate. What a delightful surprise to discover a deposit of more than $1,200 I had failed to record the first week I was responsible! God knew I had the money I needed, but He kept me from remembering it. If I had known it was there, I might have used it for less-needed payments without remembering that taxes were coming due.

Twice more while my husband and daughter were gone, God showed me He knew my needs better than I. Unexpectedly one day I received several hundred dollars more than I thought was needed. But God knew the bills were also going to total several hundred more than I thought they would. I had enough.

"God, where is the money for these bills?" I fretted another day. Yet even before I finished totaling the stack, God reminded me that one company regularly sent us a payment on the tenth of the month. That would more than cover current needs. I had forgotten about that payment, but again I thanked Him that all bills could be paid completely and on time.

God may answer our prayers in different ways at different times. But during those weeks of my special need, I was thankful for His speedy answers which eased my tendency to fret. He assured me He is in control.

Before they call I will answer; while they are still speaking I will hear.

Isaiah 65:24

Why Fret Figuring It Out?

DENISE HARTMAN GODWIN

Driving between my office and a client's location, I was mentally sorting out how to pay for the bills. "If that check came in from the article, and we wait to pay that other bill until next Friday, unless . . . " and so fretting filled my mind. Along the way I would intersperse, "Please, Lord, let that check come," or "Lord, help us."

My husband and I had never had extra money, but in eight years, we'd always managed somehow. Sometimes in seemingly miraculous ways, we'd have just enough to get to the next pay period. But each time I would be figuring it out all the way.

I've always had this habit of fretting about how the Lord will fix my circumstances. "Lord, if only you would do this . . . ." I would figure out the solution and present it to Him. Too often I would try to go to work to make it happen in my human strength. Self reliance to the rescue, although I never called it that.

On that warm day driving my car across town, I was brought up short by the Holy Spirit tapping me on the shoulder. God had been dealing with me on financial issues, through sermons and Bible verses I was hearing. We were earning more money than we had for a few years and yet I continued on the same mental mathematical acrobatics "making sure" we could make it.

I had to admit my maneuverings were worry and they were wrong. They symbolized doubt. Doubt that God could continue to make things work out; He must need my help to figure it out. The Holy Spirit checked my human impulses. I repented, not for the first or the last time, but sincerely for my doubt. I hadn't realized that I was doubting God in my fretting.

Now, waiting in line at the grocery store, I don't have to stew over which bills to pay. I've learned I'm wasting time that I could use to praise the Lord. Waiting in line or driving across town is a moment to say "Thank you Lord, You're doing great things."

But blessed is the man who trusts in the LORD, whose confidence is in him.

Jeremiah 17:7

Why Fret Trivial Decisions?

SHERI RYAN

When my husband and I were engaged, we found ourselves arguing over many trivial decisions. Registering for our wedding gifts presented the most disagreements. *I* wanted fancy glasses and *he* wanted sturdy ones. *He* wanted plates with fruit or vegetables in the center, whereas *I* preferred the design to be displayed around the outer edge. Decisions like these caused us to wish that this process would soon be over!

On one particularly long day of registering, we were extremely exhausted. We were in the bed and bath section of a department store picking out towels. This was one area in which I assumed we could agree. How could we go wrong with towels? How wrong I was! We had already agreed upon the colors for our house, so I began choosing burgundy and hunter green bath towel sets. Then Shawn explained that he preferred light colored towels because the dark ones leave visible balls of fuzz on his skin.

I wanted to scream out of frustration! Instead of losing my temper, I started laughing hysterically! How ridiculous we were! Soon, we were both laughing at our foolishness.

We realized we had been fretting about all the little things when we needed to be focusing on what really mattered—our future life together. Our towels, glasses, and dishes were not really important. We were about to join our lives together forever. We knew that God would take care of the little things in our lives as well as guide us through any difficult trials we may face.

In the end, we compromised on the towels and registered for *white* plates. I look at all these gifts now and laugh. All that really matters in the scheme of things is that God brought us together for a reason. Our wedding presents may break or wear out, but our love will always remain. Keeping that thought guards against fretting the trivial things.

Do not store up for yourselves treasures on earth, where moth and rust destroy, and where thieves break in and steal. But store up for yourselves treasures in heaven, where moth and rust do not destroy, and where thieves do not break in and steal. For where your treasure is, there your heart will be also.

Matthew 6:19–21

Why Fret
A Struggling Marriage?

FLORENCE LITTAUER

Having endured several years of an emotional void in my marriage, I understand women who say they've given up trying to get their partner to listen. But what I've also learned by hanging in there is that if at least the wife tries to understand her mate and develop an awareness of his needs, the marriage has a good chance of not just surviving but of thriving. If we can learn to lower our expectations of our husbands where listening is concerned and try to tune in to their style of communicating, we may stand a greater chance of being heard.

So many of the riches Fred and I now share in our marriage weren't unearthed until the last few years. After plodding along, trying to express ourselves and understand each other, we're finally at the point where the effort is paying off. Though our personalities are still opposites, we seem to be balancing the differences better. I've learned to feel and think at the deeper level that comes so naturally for Fred, and likewise, he has picked up much of my spontaneity and excitement about life. We have come in from our extremes and met in the middle.

When I look back and see how close we were to giving up on our whole relationship, I realize how critical time is in allowing us to grow, heal, and mature. I encourage any woman struggling to find emotional intimacy in her marriage to hang in there long enough to discover it. And if you had that intimacy once, then take steps to recapture it. In all probability, your husband wants to understand you and feel close to you, he just may not know how.

Wives, in the same way be submissive to your husbands so that, if any of them do not believe the word, they may be won over without words by the behavior of their wives.

1 Peter 3:1

(Pages 110–111, *Can I Control my Changing Emotions?* Annie Chapman, Luci Shaw, Florence Littauer, Bethany House Publishers, 1994. Used by permission.)

Why Fret Your Husband's Behavior?

JOAN CLAYTON

Maybe it was a result of teaching school for thirty-one years. In the classroom, behavior must be monitored constantly. Maybe it came from having had three lively, rough-and-tumble boys of our own. Certainly they had to be taught and trained in their behavior.

But when it came to changing the behavior of my husband, I began to hit a brick wall! Did I ever fret the God stuff!

I had the mistaken idea that husbands could be changed. When Emmitt did something I didn't like, my way was always better. If I persisted and stood my ground, a shouting match usually developed and I ended up with hurt feelings. I pouted the rest of the day.

After one particular episode, I was distraught. Surely I was not the one that was wrong . . . or was I? Did I want peace or did I want to continue trying to change my husband?

After much prayer, I finally relinquished my right to be right. (Even when I was right!) I simply told the Lord that I was sorry and asked Him to forgive me. I confessed that I could not control other people's behavior, especially that of my husband. After all, I fell in love with him just the way he was. Why would I want to change that?

I awakened in the night with Emmitt's arms around me and he was whispering: "Honey, I'm so sorry. I was dreaming and in my dream I heard the way I talked to you yesterday. Will you please forgive me?"

I threw my arms around my wonderful husband and silently thanked the Lord for showing me that only He can change people.

I learned a valuable lesson in the wee hours of that morning. It is one I've never forgotten. After discussing the issue, I pray and leave it in God's hands. He does the rest. Then I don't have to fret the God stuff.

May there be peace within your walls and security within your citadels.

Psalm 122:7

Why Fret
A Hardworking Husband?

JAN HOFFBAUER

I called my sister complaining, "I need your help. Mike has been working long, long hours for a month now. I miss him. I miss his cheerfulness. I even miss his watching television and not paying any attention to me."

I never thought I would complain about the television being off and the house quiet. But the long hours without him over such an extended period of time took its toll on my spirits.

"How I long for a husband to spend time with, even if only a short time," my single sister answered.

Why was I fretting the time Mike spent at work, when I knew he was working extra hours to provide a stable environment for us? I thought about all the single women I knew, including my sister. I thought about all the widows, who would open their loving arms to spend five minutes more with their deceased spouse. I thought about the friends whose marriages ended in divorce.

I did not want Mike to come home after a tedious workday to a nagging and complaining spouse, but to an understanding, compassionate, caring companion.

Instead of fussing and fretting that Mike and I were separated for a few hours, I turned to God in thanksgiving. I thanked Him for a gentle, kind, caring husband, one who loves me unconditionally, the same as my Heavenly Companion loves me. By giving my lonely heart to God, He filled that emptiness with His companionship and comfort.

. . . a quarrelsome wife is like a constant dripping.

Proverbs 19:13b

Why Fret Controlling Children?

PATTY STUMP

As a parent, I want my children to be all they can be; not *the* best, but *their* best. I want them to be kind and thoughtful, well mannered and appreciative. "Don't forget to say thank you! Use a kind voice! Watch your elbows! Play nicely! Remember to share! Work together! Smile!" are statements I frequently toss their direction. If I'm not careful, my focus zooms in on their behavior and shortcomings, and I loose sight of their hearts and potential.

Children need guidance as they grow and learn, but they also need patience and grace, laughter and encouragement; more strokes and fewer pokes! They learn the most from what they see and receive, prompting me to ask the Lord to help me be a mentor rather than a manager; to focus less on the trivial trifles and more on the tender hearts within them.

In fretting and fussing, I reveal a lot about my shortcomings to my children and little about the attributes of God. Thankfully He's at work in their lives, and mine as well, bringing about His likeness and His will in His timing; committed to fashioning them in His image rather than the mold I've created.

In reality, I can't make them what I want them to be, but I can guide them in knowing the One at work within each of us. In so doing, they'll not only grow to be their best, but His best as well!

Train a child in the way he should go, and when he is old he will not turn from it.

Proverbs 22:6

Why Fret The Empty Nest?

GEORGIA CURTIS LING

The windshield wipers slowly passed back and forth, but my vision was still watery. I couldn't blame the windshield wipers—they were doing a great job. It was the radio's fault, coupled with my inability to reach a tissue.

Driving to pick up our son from Pre-K several years ago, I listened to Dr. Dobson and his "Focus On The Family" program concentrating on the topic of the "empty nest." I wasn't close to experiencing that syndrome, but my tears let me know I realized my little guy would all too soon pry away my grip and leave the nest. Time has a way of zooming by.

As parents we want our children to grow, mature and gain independence. But I'm learning the growing pains they experience are just as painful for parents. It hurt when he held his bottle for the first time. I was so proud of his accomplishment until I suddenly realized he didn't need me like before.

I remember his first sleep-over at a friend's house. I lay awake waiting for the phone to ring. When it was silent, I kept picking it up to make sure there was a dial tone. He didn't need me. He actually had a great time without dear old mom.

Now he's in his early school years. The only tears shed on the first day of school were mine as I drove from the parking lot, yearning to turn around and keep him at home, just for one more year.

In each of those instances I was tempted to fret about his new-found step of independence, but by focusing on God's promises, my heart could continue to rely on God. Knowing that when he runs out from under my wings, a little at a time or even when he flies from the nest completely, I can pray and trust God, believing I'm releasing him into His care. He covers him with *His* feathers, and shelters him under *His* wing, the most safe and secure nesting place of all. That promise makes my heart stop fretting because God's wings are much stronger than mine.

He will cover you with his feathers, and under his wings you will find refuge; his faithfulness will be your shield and rampart.

Psalm 91:4

Why Fret Teenage Drivers?

DEBRA WEST SMITH

They never mentioned it in prenatal class. We discussed delivery and diapers, but no one warned us about the babies growing up and driving. My children are now eighteen and sixteen. The first has scored three accidents, thankfully with only a bump on her head. The youngest found a pole in the driveway, but then he's just getting started. We've been through the proper steps of drivers education and permit period; still, there's no substitute for experience.

Perhaps the Lord intends this phase as a time of spiritual growth for parents. I definitely pray more. Despite that, fretting was stealing my joy and eroding my peace. I constantly watched the clock, checked on road conditions, jumped when the phone rang, and panicked at sirens. My daughter called me paranoid.

"With good cause," I'd say.

Then our patient Father gave me a gentle nudge—with an eighteen-wheeler. While breezing along the interstate one day, the truck driver pulled into my lane without looking. One moment I was congratulating myself on finding bargains at the mall, and the next minute, "Wham!" My side mirror was gone and the truck's "lug nuts" were chewing up my door. My husband later compared it to Ben Hur's chariot race against the guy with spiked wheels!

Struggling to stay on the road, I pounded on the horn. Fortunately, the driver realized his mistake and pulled away. As we surveyed the damage, I was amazed that it was so minor. That truck was huge and the potential for disaster great. Yet the Father had sheltered me in His hand, as He has always done. And the thought occurred that the same hand holds my family.

Nothing touches us without his permission, and by then it has become His good and perfect will.

I had definitely been "fretting the God stuff" and it was time to stop.

Okay, so I still love my kids and worry about them. But the Scripture promises that "He will keep him (or her) in perfect peace whose mind is stayed on Thee." It's working.

So do not fear, for I am with you; do not be dismayed, for I am your God. I will strengthen you and help you; I will uphold you with my righteous right hand.

Isaiah 41:10

Why Fret Saying "No"?

CATHY CLARK

"Please, Mom?" My twelve-year-old daughter sat across the table from me. She took a bite of salad and turned pleading eyes toward me. "Can I see the movie?"

I sighed, searching for new words for the same answer I had given the other times she had asked to see this current popular movie.

"You don't trust me." A small pout formed on her lips.

"Trusting you has nothing to do with this. I want to protect you."

Questions like these used to be much simpler to answer when my children were younger. Now, as my daughter teetered between childhood and adulthood, she was anxious to stretch across that imaginary line. I fretted about my answers. *Am I being prudish or am I being wise?* I pleaded with the Lord for daily wisdom.

The next morning, driving to church, I noticed a house surrounded by a chain link fence. A sign on the fence said in big letters: "WARNING, GUARD DOG." Instinctively I searched for this guard dog to see what trouble an intruder might encounter. But I discovered the gate wide open and the guard dog curled up by the fence sleeping in the sun. An intruder would have no trouble walking in and doing harm.

The impact of that scene hit me with full force. Like that guard dog, I had been given the responsibility of protecting something. I wanted to guard my daughter's young heart and mind from harmful intrusion that could pervert her views of godly romance and love.

Yet, I realized, sometimes I'm tempted to curl up and sleep in the sun. I get tired. It's easy to think that by simply hanging out a sign lettered "CAUTION," the enemy will read it and go away, when actually the gate is wide open inviting him to come in.

I was convicted afresh about the importance of guarding our hearts, not only my children's, but my own as well. I have to trust the Lord daily for strength and wisdom, especially on those days when I'd rather be resting in the sun than doing my job. With renewed peace, I knew guarding my daughter's heart meant saying "no" once in awhile.

Above all else, guard your heart, for it is the well-spring of life.

Proverbs 4:23

Why Fret Control?

BETTY SOUTHARD

As the mother of three daughters, I was often driven to my knees before the Lord. Particularly as they began dating, I prayed them in and out of many relationships. Well . . . prayed, cajoled, fretted, nagged, argued, lectured, demanded, punished, counseled . . . whatever worked.

I remember one very destructive and controlling relationship in which our daughter, Heidi, was involved. I had exhausted all avenues to derail it, including sending her to Australia for summer missions.

I became impatient with God. "Lord," I cried, "if it's so clear to me how destructive this relationship is, why don't You see it too and do something about it?"

One time after a particularly upsetting phone call, I lay exhausted before the Lord. In my silence, I began to sense his presence. I recalled Jeremiah 29:11: 'For I know the plans I have for you,' declares the Lord, 'plans to prosper you and not to harm you, plans to give you hope and a future.' It was as if the Lord was quoting it to me saying: "I know the plans I have for Heidi. Will you trust her to me?"

"But, Lord," I argued, "she isn't listening to me, and I don't think she's listening to You either."

All I heard back was "Let go. Trust Me."

"I want to, Lord, but how?" I knew that God wouldn't over-rule her free will. If I stopped intervening, and the Holy Spirit didn't intervene, what might happen?

But gently, patiently, tenderly, God simply kept repeating in my mind, "I know the plans I have for Heidi." I began to cling to that promise and surrendered Heidi to the Lord. Each and every time the fears and fretful thoughts flooded my soul, I simply repeated God's promise.

Slowly, but surely, I was able to let go. While the situation hadn't changed outwardly, inwardly I was learning to stop fretting.

Eventually God did, in His time, finally give Heidi the wisdom and strength to break off that relationship. But it wasn't because of any effort on my part. In fact, I have since discovered that the more I try to control a situation, the less freedom God seems to have to work. God used Heidi's situation to teach me a lesson that has had a profound and lasting impact in my life. Why fret about changing someone, when in reality we can't change anyone, except ourselves?

Those who know your name will trust in you, for you, LORD, have never forsaken those who seek you.

Psalm 9:10

Why Fret Family Communication?

CHARLES SWINDOLL

I vividly remember some time back being caught in the undertow of too many commitments in too few days. It wasn't long before I was snapping at my wife and our children, choking down my food at mealtimes, and feeling irritated at those unexpected interruptions through the day. Before long, things around our home started reflecting the pattern of my hurry-up style. It was becoming unbearable.

I distinctly recall after supper one evening the words of our younger daughter, Colleen. She wanted to tell me about something important that had happened to her at school that day. She hurriedly began, "Daddy-l-wanna-tell-you-somethin'-and-I'll-tell-you-really-fast."

Suddenly realizing her frustration, I answered, "Honey, you can tell me . . . and you don't have to tell me really fast. Say it slowly."

I'll never forget her answer: "Then listen slowly."

I had taken no time for leisure. Not even at meals with my family. Everything was uptight. And guess what began to break down? You're right, those all-important communication lines.

God not only made man. He talked with him, He listened to him. He considered His creature valuable enough to spend time with, to respond to. It took time, but He believed it was justified.

There are entire books written on communication, so I'll not be so foolish as to think I can develop the subject adequately here. I only want to emphasize its importance. It is imperative that we understand that without adding sufficient leisure time to our schedule for meaningful communication, a relationship with those who are important to us will disintegrate faster than we can keep it in repair.

Take time to listen, to feel, to respond. In doing so, we "imitate God" in our leisure.

Everyone should be quick to listen, slow to speak and slow to become angry.

James 1:19b

(Pages 163–164, *Stress Fractures*, by Charles Swindoll, Zondervan Publishing House, MI, 1990. Used by permission.)

Why Fret Mismatched Clothes?

LYNELL GRAY

My co-worker came into work frazzled and frustrated. "She does this every morning," she complained, referring to her six-year-old. "We agree the night before on what she'll wear, then in the morning, she won't put it on!"

I smiled, remembering my own strong-willed daughter. She, too, had had very strong ideas about what she would and would not wear.

"You know, Sandie, I went through the same thing with my daughter. She loved bright colors. She consistently wanted to wear red and orange together, or purple and red. She'd put on all these wild colors and mix patterns as well. Even on Picture Day! But you have to choose your battles. I decided not to fret this one."

I could see my story had not convinced Sandie.

"The funny thing is," I continued, "my daughter ended up being the family artist. She has a natural flair for design and color. Maybe giving her that freedom allowed her to develop her abilities in that area. That was sixteen years ago! Now I'm glad I didn't make a big deal about what clothes she put on when she was six. Somehow it just doesn't seem that important any more."

Sandie still looked doubtful. Knowing that there is no one right way to parent, I made just one last comment. "However you decide to handle it, the important thing is to make sure it doesn't turn your house into a war zone. It's just not worth it. And she'll get better at making decisions as she has more practice."

I walked away reflecting on how hard we try to get our loved ones to feel and think a certain way. I thought, *Wow . . . Just think about how patient God is with us! He waits for the spiritual growth process to work in us toward the godliness He desires. We, too, need to step back and allow time for growth in others. God will work it in them, so we need to stop trying to do it ourselves!*

Even Jesus had to go through this growth process. God will work that growth in the ones we love—if we just don't fret the God stuff.

And Jesus grew in wisdom and stature, and in favor with God and men.

Luke 2:52

Why Fret About
A Child's Singleness?

LIBBY C. CARPENTER

"Is your daughter married yet?" an acquaintance asked as we met for lunch recently. I responded with my usual well-rehearsed, "No, but she's happy!" The truth is, Amy is happy, but for a long time I was not.

Since our two daughters were small I prayed almost daily for them to have Christian husbands. My older daughter, Lisa, married just after college. A fine Christian young man, her husband fulfilled all my requirements.

Two years later, our other daughter, Amy, graduated from college and moved back home. She stayed for six years. Then God answered her prayers—not for a husband—but for a job change. She would be working in a Christian ministry and living in a nearby city.

In the meantime, I continued my waiting prayer. I felt God would answer because of my persistence. As added insurance, I urged Amy to pray for the right husband. I frustrated her with books, tapes, magazine articles and newspaper clippings.

I finally asked my women's prayer group to pray for Amy. After the meeting a friend shared her unhappy experience of being married to one who appeared to be the perfect mate, but turned out to be abusive. For the first time I began to rethink the motives behind my prayers. Later at a retreat, a pastor explained that true happiness does not depend on outward circumstances, but results from an inner peace with God. It was obvious I had equated marriage with happiness.

Only when I understood how wrong I had been and admitted it to God, was I able to give up my will and relinquish Amy to Him. And do you know what happened? Genuine peace flooded my very being as I realized God is in control and He will accomplish what is best for her, whether she marries or remains single. I am now content watching my happy and loving daughter as she seeks to serve Christ at work and in her church.

I have learned the secret of being content in any and every situation.

Philippians 4:12b

Why Fret Over The Negative?

FLORENCE GRANTLAND

"Lord, do something." This was my prayer for years regarding my son. He had made some bad choices in his life and now we were seeing the fruit of what he had sown.

I tried punishing him, taking away privileges, talking sense into him, nothing worked. His behavior grew worse, and our relationship was more strained with each new episode. He just kept walking down that broad way that leads to destruction.

The stress began to affect my marriage, job, and health. I needed to cut the cord and let him assume the consequences for his actions.

After living with this problem for so long, I became negative and fretted about everything. I expected him to get in trouble. I saw in everything he did the potential for trouble. I had nursed, rehearsed, and relived every hurt and every fear until I could see no hope for him.

One day I began to write positive things about him. Entitling it "Positive Things About My Negative Son," I turned those negative statements around. Instead of saying, "He is always looking for friends to get in trouble with," I began to say, "He is using wisdom in seeking out good friends." In every situation I looked for some glimmer of hope, thanking God for the man he was going to become, believing for only good things in his future.

I prayed for the "mantle of manhood" to fall on him, for wisdom and maturity to be manifested in his life. I prayed for a wife to share in the good things God was about to do.

God has honored those prayers, although it has taken time. He is married to a lovely woman and is maturing. Each time I talk to him, I see fruit and the blessings from those seeds of hope planted years ago.

Giving him over to God and expecting Him to act was the turning point. Our relationship is healing and he is on the narrow way now.

If each of us will turn our thinking around and really believe God can change any situation, He will. Fretting only sows negative seeds. We can expect good things from God because He is the giver of every good and perfect gift.

And hope does not disappoint us, because God has poured out his love into our hearts by the Holy Spirit, whom he has given us.

Romans 5:5

Why Fret Compliments?

JERI CHRYSONG

"Say, Mom, with your calves, you look like you can squat tons!" my teenager Luc yelled from the garage.

"Thanks," I replied, "Just what every woman wants, ton-squatting calves."

"I meant it as a compliment, Mom!"

"I know, honey, I know." I smiled, thinking this compliment ranks right up there with my Sammy's, "My mom is bigger than your dad and she's gonna beat him up!" compliment of 1989, and Luc's backhanded, "A lot of moms have nice clothes and drive really hot cars, but you're the only mom I know who can put together bunk beds with a screwdriver as your only tool" compliment of 1993.

I received my first complimentary gem from pre-schooler Sammy who said, "I love you more than infinity, and past New York!" I marveled at his eloquence. Now, I'm not whining, really, but today, their compliments are phrased in sports terminology; the eloquence is gone. I fear they will never learn the art of complimenting, and I've already started apologizing to my future daughters-in-law for their lack of that art and my failure to teach it.

Yet, Jesus often spoke in terms we don't comprehend but which the people of His day did. Apparently, being called a sheep or a dog was not such a bad thing. Today, we would be insulted. I guess you just have to know the "lingo" to gain the proper perspective and discern a compliment's meaning.

Like being called "bigger than your dad and she'll beat him up" is not a weight issue, but a statement that my son believes I can protect him. And not having nice clothes or a hot car, but being able to put together a bunk bed with only a screwdriver is a tribute to my cleverness. And having ton-squatting calf muscles is high praise, indeed, from a weight lifter!

While I treasure my sons' creative and heart-felt compliments, I try not to fret about eloquence, for, at the appropriate time, their Heavenly Father will inspire them with beautiful words of love as he did King Solomon. And some day, I'll be joined by two discerning young ladies with bulging calf muscles who will be elated to find themselves loved "more than infinity and past New York."

All beautiful you are, my darling; there is no flaw in you . . . You have stolen my heart with one glance of your eyes . . .

Song of Songs 4:7, 9b

Why Fret Parenting?

JANIE NESS

The newborn separates from the umbilical cord, the curious toddler explores his world, friends gain the attention during the primary years, and finally, the flowering teenager!

Kids can't hurry and grow up. From the moment the umbilical cord was severed, I've been mindful to give my three children the liberty to mature in a timely manner. Without the Vine, Jesus Christ, I'm certain they would be on a different course. Now it's my privilege to escort my three teens through to completion during these complex years.

I'm continually reminded of their source of maturation and where mine comes from as well. When they stray or question my judgment, I do what I've been called to do: be their Mother and sunlight, not their God. In addition to being present in all seasons, it's through love and prayer that I readjust their boundary lines, allowing the natural process to occur. At times, that's joyful and sometimes unpleasant. Regardless of the circumstances, even through five years of single parenthood, I like to say, "A mother is sunlight for growth, the Son is light for truth."

Sometimes I fret whether they're on track, and occasionally, I question whether I'm fulfilling my assignment. But invariably my heart is comforted, knowing as a stay-at-home mom, I'm exactly where God wants me. He reassures me that all things work together for their good.

At moments, raising children is like clutching the wind, but when I hear my 18-year-old son vigorously pursuing his God-given talent in music, or when I peek in on my 17-year-old daughter faithfully reading her Bible late at night, I pause with silent gratitude. They are maturing from the inside out like a peach in the hot sun. The timely, vine-ripened fruit is far superior to the orangy, tough skin and airy taste of the hurried greenhouse imitation.

My youngest daughter, fourteen, surprised me with a taste of the vine's sweetness the other day. After teasing her about a comment she made involving her style of clothes, she responded with a witty reply. I chuckled, telling her she sounded like a parent.

"I learned from the best," she said, smiling.

Jokingly, I remarked, "Then if we're the best, where's our blue ribbon?"

Her head tilted. "Me," she said softly.

We've come a long way since the umbilical cord. Harvesting season is nearing, but why fret that God stuff? He's the Master Gardener who's brought us this far, forever linked through the Vine.

Remain in me, and I will remain in you. No branch can bear fruit by itself; it must remain in the vine.

John 15:4

Why Fret School Assignments?

GAYLE URBAN

"It's got to be at least 200 words, Mom! And it's due *tomorrow*!" Big brown eyes beseeched me as my son makes his latest dire need known. He's never written such a long history essay before and it's obvious that he's hit a mental wall. Reference books and crumpled paper clutter the kitchen table. He's a capable fifth grader, but this new task overwhelms him. "Mom! I can't do this!"

My emotions are mixed. I'm glad he's asking for help, but exasperated that it's on such short notice! *Why didn't he begin this a week ago?* I fret. *We could've brainstormed over the weekend and gotten a head start.* Instead, I feel the looming pressure of his deadline.

Impatience at this point will only aggravate the situation. Breathing a prayer, I begin to walk him through the assignment. Once we begin discussing the topic, it's evident that he has some basic concepts and I encourage him to write those down. Then he begins the second paragraph and drops his pencil.

"This is lousy! Look—it stinks!" In all fairness, the last sentence *was* pretty lousy.

I say as much, gently.

"See, I told you I couldn't do it," he retorts, but at least he's listening to me. I told him the truth and he respected that.

Taking a step further, I encourage him, "How can you say that thought in a different way? What does 'he worked very, very, very, hard' *really* mean?"

He pauses, challenged. Tentatively, he says, "Work was important to the man."

"That's it! Exactly!" My unexpected exuberance makes us both laugh. "This is good! Now, what's the next part?"

His essay unfolds in fits and starts, until finally, Hallelujah! 207 words.

"I did it!" my son sighs.

"You had it in you all the time!" I say, hugging his tired shoulders. He feels great and so do I.

And for an instant I see those many times when it's me crying out to the Lord, fretting, "I can't do this, Lord! Help me! Everything's a mess!" And I'm reminded of the steadfast way that He meets me with new hope, with timely resources, yes, even at the 11th hour! He is a patient teacher, and I'm grateful for the lessons.

But in their distress they turned to the LORD, the God of Israel, and sought him, and he was found by them.

2 Chronicles 15:4

Why Fret Daily Squabbles?

JANICE STROUP

My sixteen-year-old son slammed the door and stomped through the house to the kitchen where I was working. His jaw was clenched and his eyes shot sparks. He hotly explained the current problem with my other sixteen-year-old son, his twin.

I had already heard the complaint. The guys share an old car which belonged first to their grandma, next to their dad, then was passed down to their older brother. Now it belongs to two young men who have always had to share.

At times throughout their lives, the twins have argued and contended over things their dad and I don't have answers for—like whose turn it is to go first, who gets the biggest piece, who gets to sit in the front seat, and hundreds of other situations that are important to children.

At these times, we quote Proverbs 16:33 about casting lots. We ask them if they agree to let God decide and then we flip a coin. They are always satisfied with their answer.

So I calmly listened to my angry son. When he had said it all, I asked him if we could flip a coin to decide whose turn it was for the car. He grunted and nodded.

When the other twin arrived, I asked him if he would agree to flip a coin over the car decision. He said yes. The coin went into the air, the call was made, and the angry twin lost. Later I asked him if it was O.K. with him about the car.

"Yeah," he answered. "I know I lost because of my bad attitude."

What a blessing to me not to have to be upset over daily squabbles! I don't have to get emotionally involved over unanswerable questions. I simply leave the decision to Someone who knows all the answers, and loves my sons even more than I do.

The lot is cast into the lap, but its every decision is from the LORD.

Proverbs 16:33

Why Fret Releasing Our Children?

PATTY STUMP

It was 1:30 Christmas morning when a peculiar abdominal discomfort aroused me from a restless sleep. I slipped out of bed and paced the darkened house before collecting a few necessities and waking my husband with the news that I was in labor.

Over the next hours, nurses, monitors, cramps, warm blankets, doctors, and more cramps came and went. I never imagined how stretching these hours would be! At 5:35 p.m. our daughter arrived. Soft tufts of auburn hair set off her fair skin and delicate features. She was beautiful! Repeatedly I thanked the Lord for this wonderful Christmas and for the gift of our little Elisabeth.

As I cuddled Elisabeth the next morning, her body seemed lethargic and unresponsive; her eyes gray and cloudy. We anxiously looked on as medical personnel monitored her tiny body. "Do something Lord! *Please*!" I cried.

In the midst of these moments I welcomed a visit from our friend, Miss Florence. Though well into her years, she radiated a youthful glow and unshakable confidence. She listened attentively then firmly gripped my hands in hers, bowed, thanked the Lord for creating Elisabeth, and for *sharing* her with us! She asked Him to help us trust Him and entrust Elisabeth to Him, acknowledging that she was shared with us for a season of time that only He knew.

She was right. I needed to entrust Elisabeth to the Lord and to trust Him with her life; no strings attached. "Help me, Lord," I whispered, "to leave her in your hands."

It's difficult to let my children go beyond my realm of protection. I can become fretful regarding opportunities and obstacles they might encounter. Often I fear for their safety and worry concerning peer influences. Yet only God can be with them every step of the way.

Our daughter Elisabeth turned seven this Christmas and continues to blossom into a captivating gal with an enthusiastic faith. Both Elisabeth and our son T.J. are daily wrapped in my prayers as I commit them afresh to the Lord for whatever He has in store. In those moments when I want to grab them back, I am reminded that the days and ways of their lives are His, and that I must trust Him and entrust them to Him, with no strings attached.

Yet you brought me out of the womb; you made me trust in you even at my mother's breast.

Psalm 22:9

Why Fret A Difficult Child?

KAREN HAYSE

Janet's sparkly-eyed eight-year-old, Erin, smiled up at me as she told me about her new book. At the same time, my daughter, Melinda, glared out of the tops of her eyes, her arms crossed tightly against her body.

"Come on, Melinda, let's go," I coaxed, expecting her to resist my directions as she had done most of the day. Instead, she obediently followed me out the door, though her folded arms still formed an angry barrier between us. I breathed a sigh of relief. At least she obeyed this time.

The drive home was silent and tense. My mind relived the conflicts we had experienced the past day. Why couldn't Melinda be more like Erin? I looked over at her, not liking what I saw. I felt like snapping at her, berating her for all the grief she had caused. I glanced in the rear-view mirror and discovered that my face held the same sour expression as hers. "Dear God, I can't deal with this child much longer. Please help me," I fretted.

"Melinda *is* like Erin," God planted in my mind. "Remember all the beautiful qualities she has, Karen. Your unforgiveness will not make her any more ready to show them."

I pictured my daughter giggling as she tells her creative stories at the dinner table. I saw her holding the babies at the nursery with gentleness and love. An image of Melinda giving me a hand-made card flashed through my memory. Though I still felt frustrated, I reached over and patted her on the leg. "We have had a tough time, but I still think you're the greatest kid on the planet!"

Instantly, her expression softened, her arms uncrossed to grasp my hand in hers. Suddenly, she was my lovely little girl again.

Though Melinda is responsible for her own choices, I have come to realize that sometimes she lives up to my perception of her also. My gentle touches help her feel accepted and loved. Reminders that she is likable, talented, and special empower her to focus on those strengths. The more quickly I submit to Christ's spirit of unconditional love, the faster the stress and frustration of parenting melts away. Fretting is replaced by encouragement.

If anyone has caused grief . . . you ought to forgive and comfort him, so that he will not be overwhelmed by excessive sorrow. I urge you, therefore, to reaffirm your love for him.

2 Corinthians 2:5a, 7, 8

Why Fret Teenage Struggles?

CLAIRE V. SIBOLD

Our youngest child is a teenager and just beginning to test us as parents. This is an attempt on her part to gain power and control, and, yes, to become more independent. We have slowly let out the reins, giving her more and more responsibilities commensurate with her age and capabilities.

She is not particularly helpful in the morning as we try to get out the door, on our way to her school and my office. Part of her testing includes ignoring me as I call out, "It's time to leave. We're going to be late!"

She replies, "I'll be there in just a minute!"

Five, but more often ten minutes later, she emerges from her room. Most often the traffic has not been such that we have been late. We've "lucked out." Perhaps God lightened the traffic so that we managed to pull into the parking lot on time.

Because we have most often been on time, my daughter sees this as a signal to continue her ways. What often grovels me is that her room is left in shambles, her bed sometimes unmade. In the grand scheme of things, her tardiness is as she puts it, "not a big deal." However, as parents, we look beyond today; we also regard her tardiness as a lack of courtesy.

Yesterday, my daughter accompanied me to the university where she attended chapel and two of my classes. We had lunch together and had a wonderful day. This morning I reached into the small refrigerator in my office for some bottled water. There in plain view was a health bar with a note. "Mommy - Here's a snack for anytime. Healthy and delicious." I had shared with her the past week that I rarely have time for lunch due to my busy schedule.

This put things into perspective. Here she was so very thoughtful and showing concern for me. *Don't fret over the little things*, I thought. She's a great kid! God has planted in her a heart for others, and this time I was the recipient of her caring nature.

I can do everything through him who gives me strength.

Philippians 4:13

Why Fret Caring For Mother?

MARILYN J. HATHAWAY

Mother was a lady. I see her yet in her veiled hat and gloves, carrying her purse. When God called home her beloved but protective husband of sixty-four years, she turned, displaced and bewildered, to my sister. Under the watchful eyes of Janet and my magnanimous brother-in-law, Mother managed for a time, but finally she moved in with them. Though dwindled to four-feet-eight inches and one hundred pounds, Mother is still healthy and mobile. Call, "Let's go," and she will beat you to the car. But at ninety-five the hat is forgotten.

Life can be frustrating. She steps on the dog, spills her coffee, forgets the great-grandchildren's names, and, in Depression-era fashion, stashes food and treasures everywhere. Questions elicit one answer.

"Is that rotting tuna in your room, Mother?"

"I wondered about that."

"Why is that ant trail going into your closet?"

"I wondered about that."

"Where are your dirty socks?"

"I wondered about that," she answers, climbing into bed still half dressed.

Yeah, right. Sure you did!

"Bath night, Mother."

"Oh, do you think so?"

"When was your last bath?"

"I wondered about that."

Groans; moans; gnashing of teeth.

I call her long distance each Sunday. The conversation varies little.

"When are you coming down?"

"We were there last weekend, Mother."

"I wondered about that."

Scream!

Sometimes she senses all is not well and a tear drops from her eye.

"Don't fret, Mama! You have been with us forever and life without you is beyond comprehension. We don't mind the disruptions or confusion. We love you so. You will always be a lady."

Janet and I laugh a lot. Laughter keeps the tears at bay. The subtle turnings in the parent/child roles is a bittersweet coaster ride. We fret we will be like her, or that we won't. We fret we won't live so long, or that we will. We fret that her weight dropped or she caught a cold. We fret; but God alone has numbered her days—and ours.

Do not despise your mother when she is old. May your father and mother be glad; may she who gave you birth rejoice!

Proverbs 23:22b, 25

Why Fret Bachelorhood?

MAX LUCADO

In our culture we have certain things that we simply don't know how to handle: nuclear reactors, inflation, pornography, and perhaps the most confusing of all, single people.

Single people. What an enigma! Those unusual creatures without wives or husbands. What do you say to them? How can you carry on a conversation with people who are so deprived and socially amputated? Do you pity them? Encourage them? Ignore them? Our culture is built so much around the home that those without a home are . . . well, they're kind of like a plane without a hangar (high-flying, but nowhere to go in a storm).

Once, before I was married, I took a trip to visit my old alma mater. I saw a lot of old friends. Married friends, professors, ex-classmates, ministers, old girlfriends. Their response to my still-matelessness was amusing.

"Haven't found the right one yet?" they'd inquire. "Gee, Max, I'm sorry." (As though I'd failed at life.)

Some were more tactful. "How's your social life?" (What they really wanted was a scouting report.)

"Fine," I'd say. (I got a kick out of leaving them wondering.)

"Oh." They'd get nervous and then close in with something more discreet:

"What about Saturday nights?" (Wink.)

Others had pity on me. Several put their arms around my shoulders or gently took my hand (as though I were terminally ill) and confided, "God has one waiting for you, Max. Don't be afraid." (Was it my imagination or did I detect a little sympathetic rubbing on the ringless finger?)

I know people mean well. But, honestly . . . is bachelorhood really a disease? Are life and meaning found only at the marriage altar? Is there no room at the inn for those who sleep alone? Are they that socially underdeveloped?

Jesus suggested that singleness is more than acceptable. In fact, Jesus called it a gift (Matt. 19:12); not for everybody but for a few. A gift that encourages "undivided devotion to the Lord" (1 Cor. 7:35). Perhaps, then, a single Christian should not be regarded as one who is spiritually impotent but as one who is gifted. I was grateful for my "gift" of singleness. Later God chose to replace my gift with a wife. I'm thankful, and I'm still serving him. But, believe it or not, it is possible to be content and come home to an empty apartment.

Being mateless is not nearly as bad as it's made out to be. In fact, it could be part of a plan.

Are you married? Do not seek a divorce. Are you unmarried? Do not look for a wife.

1 Corinthians 7:27

(Pages 129–131, *On the Anvil*, Max Lucado, Tyndale House, 1985. Used by permission.)

Why Fret About The Neighbor's Perfect Yard?

ELIZABETH COLEMAN

"Why does neighbor Dawn's yard always look so nice, and our yard doesn't?" my five-year-old observed.

My husband and I exchanged looks. We had just spent our entire Saturday morning pulling weeds, cutting grass, and doing general spring clean up. Even then, we had barely scratched the topsoil. With my five and three-year-old "helping" me, I had spent most of my time adjusting bike helmets and retrieving balls from the street. My husband had spent nearly the first hour searching through the calf-high grass to insure that he would not puree any shovels, cars or hockey sticks. When I had hung up my gardening gloves, it was not because of a great sense of accomplishment, but because my six-month-old was up from his nap and it was lunch time.

I sighed, knowing I would never make it outside again today. I looked over at Dawn's yard. Fresh bark, carefully placed, surrounded the shrubs and covered the flower beds. Each bush was meticulously pruned, selected for size and color by her landscape designer. Dividing Dawn's yard from mine was scalloped cement edging, chosen by her designer not so much for aesthetic beauty as for its ability to keep my weeds out.

"Well, neighbor Dawn spends a lot more time in her yard than we do," I explained to Joshua.

Josh replied, "Y'know Mom, neighbor Dawn doesn't have any kids. Maybe that's why her yard looks so good."

I continually fight the inner need to have my house and yard perfect. Sometimes I give in to my perfectionistic tendencies and turn on the television set, plunk the children in front of it and tell them, "Mommy needs to . . . . " Yet, it's still my goal to be like the Mary of the Bible who loved sitting at Jesus' feet. Although I'll still need to maintain the house and yard, my first priority focuses on what is important right now, my children. As neighbor Dawn so aptly put it, "You'll have lots of time in the future to have a perfect house and yard. The only time you'll have your children is now."

Every time I start to fret about how my yard looks in comparison to Dawn's, I remember her words and make a fresh commitment to be like Mary, choosing the better things of life.

But seek first his kingdom and his righteousness, and all these things will be given to you as well.

Matthew 6:33

Why Fret Insignificance?

SHARON HANBY-ROBIE

This morning as I was making my usual walk-laps around the local roller rink, I found myself suddenly dodging multiple exercise mats and gym bags. Apparently, they are now conducting aerobics classes at the same time "open walking" is scheduled. I found myself getting really annoyed. My walking partner took it all in stride. I'm sure she wondered why I reacted the way I did.

This got me thinking. It's amazing how easily we can be annoyed and angered with such simple, insignificant events of life. Even more amazing to me is the fact that whenever I have found myself going through a particularly difficult time in life, the little things don't annoy me. It seems that when my perspective is changed and all my energy is focused on a more important situation, I am able to manage the little annoyances with ease.

I found this an interesting revelation. Another lesson to be learned—again. God must be very patient with me because He graciously continues to teach me over-and-over again the same lessons. He faithfully supported me through many difficult trials. Loving and caring for me. Guiding me with gracious grace. His continuous gentle Spirit reminds me to learn again that if He can be trusted in the "big" things, He certainly can be trusted with the "little" annoyances of life.

I should have responded with a smile and let His Spirit shine this morning. Instead, I allowed my own aggravated attitude to cloud the day. Next time, I'm not going to fret the insignificant things!

Trust in the LORD with all your heart and lean not on your own understanding; in all your ways acknowledge him, and he will make your paths straight.

Proverbs 3:5–6

Why Fret Frustration?

KATHY COLLARD MILLER

My friend from the Midwest often calls me to air her grievances about her husband. She just can't understand why he doesn't look at life the same way she does. He's more of a controlling kind of person and she's more relaxed about life. He wants to tell their children exactly what to do and she likes them to discover their own way. "Kathy," she moans, "why can't he see that they need to grow in their own way? He makes me so mad! When is he going to see the light?"

She may not be telling the right person about her problem because I can see both points of view. As I try to share the value of his perspective, I feel frustrated as she dismisses my comments.

As I hung up the phone after our last conversation, I muttered, "Why can't she give him the same slack she gives her kids? When is she going to see the light?"

I immediately burst out laughing! I was getting frustrated with my friend because I couldn't make her see my point. She was getting frustrated with her husband because she couldn't make him see her point. He was getting frustrated with the children because he couldn't make them see his point. What a cycle! Everybody is intent on changing everybody else and not applying a healing balm of grace!

As I look at my own relationships, I can see how much I try to make other people change their opinions. I'm trying to be their Holy Spirit! Talk about fretting the God stuff!

Of course, I have the privilege of sharing my opinion, but as soon as I try to change them, I'm fretting! And I'm stepping into God's realm. Of course, there are times when we need to take firm action if there's abuse or addictions. But most of the time, in the everyday things of life, we need to let God move in the people we love. That's trusting God for the big and small stuff! I'm going to make a fresh commitment to let Him do what He's best at.

All of us who are mature should take such a view of things. And if on some point you think differently, that too God will make clear to you.

Philippians 3:15

Why Fret Communication?

LUCI SWINDOLL

In my mind, successful communication requires two elements that many in the working world neglect: knowing how to talk and knowing how to listen. Sounds simple enough, doesn't it, but it's more difficult than it sounds. In a sense, there's an art to it. Generally, people love to exchange light, easy conversation. They like to laugh and joke and feel relaxed. It has been my experience that employees or colleagues respond more readily and favorably to a supervisor or leader who can make small talk with them. Lee Iacocca, bestselling author and Chief Executive Officer of Chrysler Corporation, puts it so well, "You don't succeed for very long by kicking people around. You've got to know how to talk to them, plain and simple."

That's the secret: plain and simple. Breaking the ice! It can seem, on occasion, like a waste of time, yet it has the power to open doors to serious discussions and vital brainstorming.

When words are many, sin is not absent, but he who holds his tongue is wise.

Proverbs 10:19

(Page 93, *After You've Dressed For Success*, by Luci Swindoll, Word, 1987.)

Why Fret
Growth Speed Limits?

MARGARET PRIMROSE

Past ninety and living in a nursing home, Grandma S. really did not want to use a walker. She felt drawn to pray about the demands of an aging body.

Sandra also had a problem with age. She wanted to start school, but her mother said she had to have another birthday first. In frustration, Sandra burst out, "Bake my cake and give me my birthday now."

Just like Grandma and Sandra, we all could benefit from praying, "Lord, help me to live by the inch." Probably most of us think we would rather be at some other "inch" of life than where we are.

A young teen chafes for the day he is old enough for a driver's license. At sixteen, he frets about earning money for a car to go with his new license.

A childless wife yearns for a family. Later, when she does have to cope with a toddler, she wishes she could get a good night's sleep. At long last her baby graduates from high school, and she broods in her empty nest.

One man can hardly wait for retirement. Another is bored with it from the start.

The fact is that Grandma S. and her recently-retired daughter were enjoying renewed camaraderie. Sandra was actually in her most carefree days and the young mother in her most fulfilling years. The man longing for retirement is often at the peak of his career, and the new retiree may be forgetting dreams he planned to pursue.

When St. Paul was in prison, he wrote that he had *learned* to be content in all circumstances. What an example he is for those of us who fret about our "speed limits" or tend to focus on the "rear-view mirror" rather than glance into it.

This is the day that the LORD has made; let us rejoice and be glad in it.

Psalm 118:24

Why Fret Interruptions?

MARJORIE K. EVANS

Oh, no, I thought as the telephone rang for the third time that busy Friday morning. *I'll never get to Bible study on time.*

It was Katy returning my call from the day before. I had phoned to see how her husband was getting along. On Tuesday he had had surgery for a large aneurysm and was still in intensive care.

Katy related he was making fair progress but was still in a lot of pain. Then she reported each minute detail of his operation. After that she told all about the surgery he had gone through months earlier. As Katy went on-and-on, I began to feel impatient and wondered how I could end the conversation.

Then suddenly I remembered what a friend in our Bible study had told me several weeks before. She said, "I used to look at the things people did and said and if they didn't measure up to my expectations, many times I became unloving, impatient, or angry. But God showed me that I need to look at them through His eyes of love, because He sees them through the shed blood of His Son Jesus Christ."

I thought that was an excellent idea for the Lord had been making His love for others more real to me.

Since God is God, why am I fretting and why am I judging an-

other? I wondered. Then I breathed, *Forgive me, dear Lord, and let me see Katy through Your eyes of love.*

Immediately I saw a frightened woman, terrified that her 72-year-old husband whom she had loved for 50 years might not pull through. As I saw her that way, my whole attitude changed, and I listened until she completely unburdened herself.

It didn't matter that I was late to Bible study for the Lord had already taught me a beautiful lesson.

Be kind and compassionate to one another.

Ephesians 4:32a

Why Fret Perfect Hospitality?

LYNELL GRAY

We were young newlyweds just out of college and we loved to entertain. Already I was known as a good cook. One day as I scurried around making sure everything was perfect in preparation for our guests, that still, small voice stopped me cold. "Who," it asked, "do you want them to be impressed with?"

"What?"

"Who do you want them to be impressed with—you or Me?"

I stammered within myself, "Well, You, of course, Lord . . . ." Yet, in that moment, I realized that wasn't true. "Oh, Lord, I thought I was just being a good hostess, but I see that being perfect is a matter of pride. Help me to relax and let You be the one to shine."

Slowly it dawned on me why we seldom got invited to our friends' homes. Our friends were young couples like us. Occasionally, an impressed male friend would turn to his young wife and say something like, "Why don't you make salad like this?" I was unwittingly intimidating these young women with my obsession for perfection.

As I allowed myself to keep a less-than-perfect house and fix a less-than-perfect gourmet meal for guests, I found that, not only did we get invited over to others' homes, but I enjoyed myself more without my unnecessary standard of perfection.

God is the only perfect One. What a relief it was when I let God be God, and let myself be human! It's much easier when I don't fret the God stuff.

Nobody should seek his own good, but the good of others.

1 Corinthians 10:24

Why Fret A Mess?

DURLYNN ANEMA-GARTEN

While I've never been a fanatic about cleanliness and neatness, I do abhor too much mess. My husband is worse. He loves an orderly yard.

Therefore, we were in shock when we arrived at our second home on California's North Coast. Two months previously we had rented by phone the basement of our house to a couple who were building on the street above us. We agreed either from a sense of compassion—or perhaps from greed.

Little did we know their building project would encompass our small piece of land. Wood littered the entire lot with piles of lumber stacked several feet high. My pitiful attempt at landscaping was crushed and flattened. Pipe and extra wood lay wherever the lumber stacks didn't reach.

"What in the world?" my husband yelled. He began to fret and so did I. This was supposed to be a place to relax, not fret. Yet that was what we did during the first afternoon after our arrival.

Our fretting meant we met with our renters for the first time with a disgruntled attitude. After all, "they" had ruined our peace and quiet. "They" had created this mess.

The husband who was renting didn't lessen our feelings. He insisted on telling us what he did to improve our place—new light switches, fixing a leaking bathtub (which wasn't broken previously), putting in shelves, etc. Then he added fuel to the fire by informing us of our poor construction job (which we already knew).

Talk about increased fretting! Why did we let them into our place? What a mess in our yard! What should we do?

Then the light dawned on us. What does the Bible say about Christians? Didn't Jesus tell us to demonstrate our Christianity in spite of disaster? To tolerate people with all their blemishes? Jesus tells us to serve God by serving man.

I looked at my husband and hung my head. "Maybe instead of fretting we need to pray," I said.

He nodded numbly. I know he would rather have fretted. But he did bow in prayer.

And a funny thing happened as the weekend came to a close.

We became more accepting of the mess. And then they began to clean it up!

Whoever does not love does not know God, because God is love.

1 John 4:8

Why Fret Singleness?

JENNY YOON

"It doesn't sound like he likes you very much." My friend's words sank despairingly into my heart. Although I was refuting his comments and making excuses for my date's lack of initiative, I knew I was trying to protect myself from my fear of rejection. Deep down inside, penetrating through my shield of denial, I was faced with the biting reality of my friend's comment.

Experiencing rejection comes with the territory of being a single woman. Although the experience of rejection is a natural and necessary process in finding the "right one," the sting it leaves behind is nonetheless screechingly painful to remove. During these times of inner turmoil, I question God, "Why again, God? How many frogs do I have to go through until I finally meet a prince? Will it ever happen?"

After a period of fretting with the Lord, He always seems to gently pin me down so I can be still enough to hear the truth and grace of His ways. He is revealing to me that I am His precious daughter and wants nothing but the very best for me. He desires to bring someone into my life who will love and adore me like He does. It's as if I have brought home all of my dates, but my firm yet loving Father did not approve of them. He was able to see through them in ways I was not capable of.

Although I'm tempted to fret after facing rejection and ending a relationship, my wise Father is showing me that these experiences help me grow into His image. My Abba "Daddy" is in his garage painstakingly building a "surprise" for me. When the time is right—when I have grown enough to fit into his "surprise"—He'll present it to me. Because my Daddy knows all of the complexities within me, I know I will have a gigantic smile on my face when I grab my surprise.

In the meantime, I'll continue to grow in my trust, patience, and confidence in His timing and in His ways. "Just hurry up a little bit, Daddy!"

I am not saying this because I am in need, for I have learned to be content whatever the circumstances.

Philippians 4:11

Why Fret Priorities?

GIGI TCHIVIDJIAN

In making a priority list, I have discovered it is quite important to learn to discern between the demands, expectations, and responsibilities that are real and those that are imaginary.

For example, we have quite a large yard and live in an area where almost everyone has a lawn service. We do our own mowing and trimming, and I found I became quite overwrought and demanding about the yard. I was driving everyone nuts, especially my eldest son, who is our chief gardener. There is nothing wrong in working hard in the yard. It is good for me and for my children. There is nothing wrong with having a lovely yard. In fact, it would not be good stewardship to let it go and not care. But my motivation was becoming a bit confused. I do love and enjoy a lovely, manicured lawn, but I am afraid I was pushing so hard because each time I drove home, past all the lovely lawns with the lawn-service trucks out in front, I would feel badly that my yard didn't measure up. You see, I was beginning to put my yard and its beauty before my family. It got so bad that when we sat outside in the sun, enjoying one another, I would see a few weeds and comment that they should have been pulled. I couldn't enjoy my family or my yard. Now that was an imaginary demand.

But as a wife, mother, friend, and Christian, I also have many expectations and demands that are very real and very necessary. It is not always easy to determine which ones are vital and which ones are not. Sometimes they even overlap, and I have not found an easy solution. I know I spend much of my day saying, "I have to," "I must," or "I don't have time," and I blame my being too busy on anything or anyone but myself. Often, it is true that I have to, because if I don't do it, nobody will. But sometimes (more often than I like to admit), I am too busy because I have chosen to be too busy.

There is a time for everything, and a season for every activity under heaven.

Ecclesiastes 3:1

(Pages 70–71, adapted from *A Woman's Quest for Serenity*, Gigi Tchividjian, Revell, 1981. Used by permission.)

Why Fret Hectic Schedules?

CINDY BAILEY

How was I going to get it all done? Only 2 p.m., and already frazzled, I had to cram in piano lessons and Brownies and dinner and baths and prayers before bedtime. I left one daughter at Grandma's, raced to school to pick up the other, and headed across town for piano.

Somehow we were early, which gave me ten minutes to brood about life's hectic pace on a frigid winter day.

"Can I wait outside? It's such a pretty day," my daughter asked.

"In this weather? Be my guest. You have ten minutes," I replied, feeling as cold and mean as the wind.

Within a moment, my child found a partially frozen mud puddle and delighted in its wonders. She touched it with her toes. She crunched the soft ice with her fingers. She marveled at how the warmth from her hand melted the frozen dirt.

"That was fun," she exclaimed. Her toasty smile began to melt the ice in my heart.

In those nine minutes that she found delight in one of God's wonders, I realized how my own perspective lacked a sense of delight in each day God gives me. Why fret when things are busy?

I can have a calm heart in the midst of rushing from here to there. I can replace my cold heart with the warmth of enjoying each moment God gives eyes to see and arms to hug.

The ice on that mud puddle froze again quickly after my daughter no longer disturbed it. But I was determined that the newly warmed edges of my heart would not freeze again. When I next felt fretting replacing rejoicing in God's provision of a day, I remembered my daughter enjoying a "pretty day."

. . . you will fill me with joy in your presence, with eternal pleasures at your right hand.

Psalm 16:11b

Why Fret That Proverbs 31 Woman?

VICKEY BANKS

Okay, I think I've got it. I've attended the seminars, scanned the self-help aisles, had a makeover, and conscientiously taken notes during the pastor's sermons. I've been analyzed and scrutinized. The tests have been tabulated and the results are in.

I have a Sanguine/Otter/Influencing personality. (No, I'm not schizophrenic! They're all the same—just titled differently depending on who designed the test!) My love language is quality time meaning that no matter how much my poor husband does for me, I will always want more time alone with him! My face shape is oval and I look best in fall colors. (I have been advised to rid my closet and make-up bag of all traces of fuchsia.) My spiritual gift is exhortation and I most often express it through speaking, teaching, and writing. Unfortunately, no one can find a lick of musical talent within me!

But, now that I'm starting to feel a little better about myself, I think I'll read the Bible. Oh no, there she is . . . the Proverbs 31 Woman! Within the fatal span of thirty-one verses, my self-image has been reduced to that of a gnat! The more I know about myself, the less I look like her. There's no hope. I'll never match up.

She's the original Superwoman. To quote an old television advertisement, "She can bring home the bacon and fry it up in a pan." She cooks, she cleans. She shops, she sews. She trades, she teaches. She shares, she shines. She dresses well and everybody loves her.

What's her secret? Is there a seminar I can sign up for? A book I can buy? A new shade of lipstick? A megavitamin maybe? Come on, there's got to be something!

Graciously, God whispers to my sagging spirit, reminding me that the Proverbs 31 Woman is not the standard I am to flawlessly live up to. She was King Lemuel's dream girl for his son! In fact, I am never to try to be exactly like anyone else. Rather, I am to use all that I am to accomplish what God desires.

When we fret, trying to compare ourselves to others, a syndrome called "I Disease" takes our concentration off God. I start focusing on "me"! But we'll stop fretting when we trust that God will work in us however He desires—whether or not we become like the Proverbs 31 Woman.

Nevertheless, each one should retain the place in life that God has assigned to Him and to which God has called him.

I Corinthians 7:17

Why Fret
A Least Favorite Chore?

LINDA LAMAR JEWELL

Tired and grumpy, I thumped the iron down and closed my eyes. "Oh, Lord, this is boring. My feet hurt. My back hurts. I'm tired of ironing."

When I opened my eyes, the blank wall still stared back at me. Sighing, I returned my focus to the collar of a white cotton blouse that soon reflected my rumpled attitude. In my rush to finish my least-favorite Saturday afternoon chore, I pressed in some creases while pressing out others.

A few blouses later, I glanced over my shoulder and saw the summer afternoon beckoning to me. I set the iron down again, wandered to the open patio door, and rested my eyes on the patch of green lawn beneath lazy summer clouds drifting through blue sky.

"God," I exclaimed, "Your creation is more interesting than a blank wall!"

Excited, I raced back to the ironing board and flipped it around so I could face the open patio door instead of the wall.

I now iron in my usual spot, but I've turned my feet and my

outlook 180 degrees. Without this change of viewpoint, I would have missed the small delights of watching a butterfly cotillion and chuckling at cheerful robins pirating cherries.

These days, I don't always recall what I've just ironed, but I do remember the changing seasons. Orange and yellow cosmos dance outside the patio door in response to summer's sunlight kisses. Autumn's setting sun is a stained-glass glow through the maroon ornamental crabapple tree. Quiet winter's snow outlines the garden path and springtime cheers the progress of a blossom parade.

Intrigued by the bounty of God's beauty, I feel more refreshed after ironing since I've changed my perspective. I look forward to this respite watching the ever-changing seasons. Ironing at a more leisurely pace, I also fabricate fewer new wrinkles.

While my hands are on automatic pilot, my eyes are resting on the scene the Master Gardener creates outside my own patio door. I watch God paint my personal wall-sized Monet—a forever changing exhibit of His glory.

When we're fretting about our least-favorite chores, maybe we just need to change our point of view. We can always find a blessing to thank God for, but it'll take us turning around the ironing board of our thinking.

... whatever is lovely ... if anything is excellent
or praiseworthy—think about such things.

Philippians 4:8

Why Fret Preparations?

DIANN G. MILLS

One of my sons planned to come home from the Marines for a visit. Another son announced his intentions to come home from college on the same weekend. *Hurry. Hurry. Change this bed and dust that table. Bake those special chocolate chip cookies and rush to the store for extra milk. Oh, no, I forgot to buy the boys' favorite bacon. Don't forget to vacuum every corner then mop the kitchen floor. Will I get everything done in time? Oh, what if one of them arrives earlier than expected, and my chores aren't completed?*

As my mind twisted and turned with all of the busy preparations, I picked up a small picture to dust. I couldn't help but smile. The picture was of me—eighteen months old and standing in the palm of my father's hand. I peered into the tiny face, so trusting, no fears, and perfectly content with my precarious position. It reminded me of a bird perched alone on an utmost tree branch. I studied my father standing there in our old backyard holding his daughter. Even though my little face peered out at the world, my father's eyes were fixed on me.

A tear slipped down my cheek. With all of my frets and concerns about the weekend being special for my two sons, I forgot my Heavenly Father had me perfectly secure in the palm of His hand. I needed to relax and enjoy His blessings. My sons were coming home.

I replaced the picture and tossed the dusting cloth into the washing machine. *Lord, what is really important?* I prayed. I knew it wasn't the cleaning or the grocery shopping. My sons would come regardless of the shape of their home. What they needed involved prayer for a safe journey.

Kneeling in the middle of "things," I thanked God for His love, care, and protection for my family. I thanked Him for keeping me secure in the palm of His hand when I wanted to stray.

The house didn't get vacuumed and the floor didn't get mopped, but the whole kitchen smelled of chocolate chip cookies, and my sons were safe at home.

When we focus our attention on the important things, we won't fret the unimportant.

But I trust in your unfailing love; my heart rejoices in your salvation.

Psalm 13:5

Why Fret Slow Grocery Lines?

CHARLOTTE H. BURKHOLDER

The automatic doors at the local grocery couldn't open fast enough for me. Racing against time, I had stopped for a few last minute items for my dinner guests. Hastily gathering the things I needed, I scanned the check-out aisles, looking for one with the least number of customers.

Ah, there was one, practically empty—only one person in front of me and she had only a few groceries. I wheeled my cart into the aisle, taking a deep breath in an attempt to decrease my accelerated heartbeat. *I believe I'm going to make it,* I sighed.

But why wasn't the line moving? Oh no! The one person ahead of me was an ancient little lady, hunched over her walker, buying Polident for her dentures. The Polident in her withered hand was either the wrong flavor, size, or price. Whatever, it was going to mean a trip back to the cosmetic aisle for an exchange.

Why me? I groaned. *Why do I always pick the aisle that's going to take forever—especially when I'm rushed?* Aroused impatience rose up in me like a swarm of angry bees. Body language screamed to express itself.

A sobering thought surfaced in my mind. *Some day I'll be a little old lady traveling in the slow lane and I'll need people to be patient with me. Jesus says we are to do unto others as we would have them do unto us.*

So, just calm down and be patient, I scolded myself. Following fast on the heels of the first thought came another which made the long wait a holy time. " . . . Whatever you did for one of the least of these brothers of mine, you did for Me" (Matthew 25:40).

Suddenly the slow, hobbled, little woman became the embodiment of the Lord I love. *I can wait on You, Lord,* I mused, *and count it a privilege.* Then I smiled at the little old lady. This time I knew for sure I would make it on time—not because the clock said so, but because my Lord was served.

When we're fretting because other people aren't cooperating with our time pressures, it'll help us to know that even though the Lord may slow us down, His timing is never late.

My times are in your hands . . .

Psalm 31:15a

Why Fret Overscheduling?

BILL HYBELS

I've made no secret of the fact that early in my ministry I was so overscheduled that I would often go two or three weeks without being home a single night with my family. During that time I began reading biographies of some of the great Christian leaders. Frequently, near the end of the books, the biographers recorded the leaders' answers to the question: If you could live your life over again, would you do anything differently? Almost always the response was, "I built a great ministry, but I broke the hearts of my children. I served others at their expense. I embittered them against God and against me. If I could do it over again, I'd properly balance ministry and family."

Those words, and the personal confrontations of friends who saw the course I was on, challenged me to change my schedule. I accepted the challenge and vowed I would never make my children pay for my involvement in ministry. By God's grace, and thanks to (my wife) Lynne and the men in my accountability group, I have maintained that commitment.

But what if I had been challenged too late in life? Or if I had neglected the challenge? Some of us don't have the luxury of doing better the second time around because of the shortness and uncertainty of life. Will there be regrets?

Several years ago a close friend of mine lost his only child, a twenty-four-year-old son, in a drowning accident. Shortly after the accident, I heard a tape of an interview in which his wife was asked how she coped with the death of her only child. She said, "I can live with the loss of my child because I can honestly say that I have no regrets about how I raised him. I wasn't a perfect mother, of course. But I poured time and energy and love into him from the day he was born. I have no regrets about that."

I can still remember where I was, driving down the road toward my house, when I heard those words. I squeezed the steering wheel and said, "God, that's my commitment from this day forward! I want to live every day without regret regarding my children. I want to pour everything I can into them during the short season that I have them."

Fathers, do not exasperate your children; instead, bring them up in the training and instruction of the Lord.

Ephesians 6:4

(Page 90–91, *Honest to God?* Bill Hybels, Zondervan, MI, 1990. Used by permission.)

Why Fret Intervening?

PAMELA ENDERBY

Early Monday morning, I crawled out of my pajamas and into my jogging suit to tackle dirty laundry. Sorting the whites from the colors, my friends' needs weighed heavy on my heart. A young wife suffers rejection from her husband's adulterous affair, a neighbor believes in his good deeds for salvation and an elderly friend grieves the loss of her husband. I long to rescue them from their giants of rejection, deception, and grief.

Then I spotted my husband's navy blue sweatshirt. Spills from his favorite late night snacks stained its front and reminded me of my recent visit at the nursing home.

Mildred's crumpled body slumped in her wheelchair. She wore a napkin stained with mashed potatoes and gravy. Protruding from her worn, tired skin, her knuckles resembled jagged mountains. Mildred's left leg, in a full cast, jutted out beneath a plaid flannel blanket draped over her lap.

"Do you like to sing?" I inquired.

Mildred's gravelly voice startled me when she blurted out, "What a friend we have in Jesus, all our sins and griefs to bear...Oh, what peace we often forfeit, oh what needless pain we bear, all because we do not carry, everything to God in prayer."

Alone and weighed down in my laundry room, I immediately

recognized I had been needlessly fretting over my friends' burdens. Often I interfere in God's business, trying to fix other's lives when I should keep out! Sometimes I'm too proud or too busy to ask for God's help.

This time, instead of fretting the God stuff, I knelt down on a pile of "whites" to pray. I gave their needs for comfort, salvation and healing to God.

It would be nice to be able to help every hurting person who crosses our path. But in trying, we often end up with tense muscles and a headache, along with a heartache. I'm going to make prayer a priority and trust God to intervene in other's lives as I intercede on their behalf. After all, He is the one who has the strength and ability to help them. He is our all-sufficient Provider.

Trust in the LORD and do good; dwell in the land and enjoy safe pasture.

Psalm 37:3

Why Fret Faulty Conclusions?

CATHERINE VERLENDEN

The technician had just arrived to work on my printer. "What's the weather doing out there?" I asked.

"Well," he said, "it's a real mess. Black ice. I did a 180 when I tried to turn in here."

My worst fears were confirmed. Today's lunch hour was allocated to buying the baby gift I was taking with me out of town tomorrow. Ice on the streets. Wouldn't you know! Why did our weather go crazy? Why had I waited till the last minute to buy this critical present? Why? Why?

"Lord," I prayed, "I have two hours until 11:30." I walked over to the window and lifted the metal blind slats with my thumb to get a better look. The parking lot was white now, and the stuff was still falling. I glumly returned to my desk.

Lunch break eventually arrived. I bothered the window one last time and could hardly believe what I saw! Our wild and wonderful weather patterns had been at work once more. There was not a speck of white on the pavement! I threw on my coat, grabbed my purse and took off grinning. "Lord, You've done it again."

Returning to the office, the precious gift safely bagged beside me, I said, "Lord, if I'd just wait on You, I'd save myself a lot of grief, wouldn't I? If I'd just give You a little time."

How often, I wonder, have I rushed to faulty conclusions and gone through unnecessary emotional turmoil because I've been unwilling to wait for Him? How often is my strength drained away as I fret?

If I wait, does that mean everything will turn out my way? I wish! But it does give me time to hear God and gain insight from Him.

Well, then, next time the schedule is under threat, will I panic? I hope not! I hope I'll wait on the Lord, turn to Him and say, "What are You doing, Lord? In the middle of all this, I thank You for Your sovereign wisdom and power, and for Your immense love. Grant me the grace to yield to You with thanksgiving and a soft heart. To wait. To listen. To hear Your heart."

Wait for the LORD, be strong and take heart and wait for the LORD.

Psalm 27:14

Why Fret Celebrations?

RONICA STROMBERG

My son had just been baptized, and he, my husband, and I were celebrating the occasion at a cozy restaurant with family and friends. With laughter, lighthearted voices, and the click of silverware surrounding me, I couldn't help thinking how much better this celebration was going than his birthday had.

Then I had been scurrying around our two-bedroom home weeks in advance, trying to make it presentable and wondering how we would ever squeeze twenty people into it. When the big day did arrive, I spent most of it in the kitchen, preparing food, washing dishes, and fussing over details. I saw little to celebrate and heard even less.

"Don't go to so much trouble," someone called to me from the living room.

"It's no trouble," my husband responded with a laugh.

Yeah, no trouble for you! I thought resentfully. Couldn't he help?

Suddenly, a passage of Scripture sprang to mind, opening my eyes to what I was doing: playing Martha. The tenth chapter of Luke tells of the time Jesus had gone to visit Martha at her home. While Martha had worked to serve Him, her sister Mary had sat at his feet, listening to His words.

Martha had become resentful and asked Jesus, "Lord, don't you care that my sister has left me to do the work by myself? Tell her to help me!"

Jesus had replied, "Martha, Martha, you are worried and upset about many things, but only one thing is needed. Mary has chosen what is better, and it will not be taken away from her."

How often I was guilty of being a Martha! Too often, I wanted everything to be perfect and I missed out on the most important things—the holiness of a baptism, the joy of a birthday, the warmth of family and friends.

As I now sat in the restaurant with the people who mattered most to me, I had an inner peace, knowing that this time, like Mary, I had chosen what was better.

Delight yourself in the LORD and he will give you the desires of your heart.

Psalm 37:4

Why Fret Martha's Example?

CARRIE PADGETT

I have probably sat through dozens of sermons about Mary and Martha. Mary chose the "better way" in sitting at the feet of Jesus to listen to him. I have nodded and taken notes while being told that Martha fretted needlessly and bothered Jesus with her home-making concerns.

But there was always a nagging question in the back of my mind, "Okay, but who is going to feed all those people? Who will draw the water for them? Who will make sure the house is swept?" I was meditating on this passage recently, asking God to show me *why* Mary's way was better. I saw the whole scene unfold before my eyes as if I was there.

Lazarus came home and announced, "Jesus is coming to our home tomorrow to visit. There will be lots of guests coming with him."

Mary immediately began to prepare bread and vegetables for the meal with the Master. Martha continued with her mending.

The next day Mary rose early to go draw water and sweep out the house. Martha slept a little longer than she should have.

Mary instructed the servant girls when to start roasting the meat and vegetables, and when to fill the water glasses. Martha insisted on doing her duties herself.

When the Master finally arrived, Mary's chores were done and she was free to spend the afternoon at the Master's feet. But Martha had not used her time wisely. She had not delegated any of the work and preferred to complain to the Lord about her sister.

As I schedule my day for household tasks, ministry and family commitments, I ask myself, "Am I making the best use of my time? Could this task be delegated to one of the children so that I can use the time to do something else that only I can do? Do I sleep instead of spending time with the Master?"

Now, I make sure that I follow Mary's example and choose the "better way." Instead of fretting about not having enough time for everything, I've learned that doing things *for* the Lord is not the same as being *with* the Lord.

"Martha, Martha," the Lord answered, "you are worried and upset about many things, but only one thing is needed. Mary has chosen what is better, and it will not be taken away from her."

Luke 10:41–42

Why Fret During A Walk?

SUE LANGSETH

"Hurry up, Skippy," I pleaded, tugging at his leash to pull him from still another sniffing detour on our walk around the block. Spring scents seem to bring out the Sherlock Holmes investigative abilities of my beagle-basset hound, whose nose is doggedly to the ground during these daily jaunts. On days when my "to do" list is five columns long and I am tempted to rush our walk, he seems to insist all the more on reflective pauses when his nose catches an intriguing scent. On this particular morning, as we headed home, the list of chores I needed to get done settled like a cloud over my head, obscuring my view of everything around me. I quickened my steps.

It was then Skippy discovered a scent that was cause for lingering near a tree in a neighbor's yard. Sunlight filtered through the tree's large notched leaves that clothed its branches with the fresh green of spring. Exquisite cup-shaped blossoms, orange at the base, turning to bright chartreuse on the petal tips, finished the ends of each twig to perfection. I marveled at the beauty which I had evidently overlooked on our previous walks.

Then I raised my eyes. There in the center of the tree perched a brilliant oriole, a swash of tangerine amid its verdant backdrop. I gazed, enchanted, as the bird dipped its head first into one blossom and then another. The creature paid no regard to my presence, but continued to sample the sweetness of each flower.

In that moment the cloud of chores lifted from my view. I delighted in the rare and beautiful sight, one of those little glimpses of heaven our Father occasionally gives us.

Days later all of those worrisome chores had faded from my memory. But the beauty of the oriole in the tulip tree remains with me. How many times have I missed sampling the sweetness of a glimpse of heaven because I was fretting over the tasks of the world?

Be still, and know that I am God; I will be exalted among the nations, I will be exalted in the earth.

Psalm 46:10

Why Fret Appearances?

LYNN MORRISSEY

I was "fret to be tied." I was "all stressed up with someplace to go" and nothing to wear. My husband Michael requested I accompany him to a business banquet, but I worried my clothes weren't suitable.

Having left my career to raise my daughter, my entertainment wardrobe was sadly outdated. Jeans and sweats were my current attire, so I fretted about what I'd wear to the dinner.

Although our income was tight, I constantly nagged Mike to let me purchase a new outfit. Reluctantly, he acquiesced. We compromised, agreeing I'd wear old slacks with a new beaded top.

Without time to bargain hunt, I found the right top at the wrong price.

Ouch! Though expensive, I justified the purchase. I hadn't bought a new outfit in years. I was ready for a night on the town—in style.

Arriving fashionably late, I made my grand entrance. One by one, heads turned and eyes followed as we threaded through a sea of dining tables—greeting, hugging, chatting.

As we approached the buffet spread, eyes still followed me. I was making a wonderful impression! I knew those beads had done the trick.

As I speared a boiled shrimp, Michael's secretary gently took my arm and gingerly led me aside. "Lynn, I don't know how to say this, but are you aware that what appears to be pantyhose are trailing behind your right leg?"

She was right! A pair of pantyhose slithered from my pant leg like some discarded snake skin. Now that the "snake was out of the bag," I slithered away in embarrassment to the ladies room.

What had happened? I must have hurriedly undressed the last time I wore the pants and removed both pants and pantyhose simultaneously. I hadn't bothered to separate the worn hose.

God allowed me to trip over my pantyhose to remind me that pride easily raises its ugly head before a fall. Fretting about my appearance hadn't made me one iota more beautiful in His eyes. He desires I wear beautiful attitudes instead.

Throughout the "new clothes" ordeal, I hadn't once looked inside my heart to remove "worn," ugly attitudes vented at my husband. These, far more than outdated clothes, marred my appearance and personality.

I rejoined Michael with a lighter, lovelier step, free from dragging around bad attitudes that promised to trip me up every time.

The Lord does not look at the things man looks at. Man looks at the outward appearance, but the Lord looks at the heart.

1 Samuel 16:7(b)

Why Fret Idealistic Expectations?

PAT PALAU

Several years ago I struggled with cancer. I had discovered that lump and I was sure it was the end. The ensuing chemotherapy nearly made me wish it were the end! I was sick and tired of feeling weak and moody. I wasn't at all the person I wanted to be.

Then I rediscovered Hebrews 12. Jesus wasn't telling me, "Run faster! You're not doing a good job!" Instead, He was encouraging me in my race. My loving Father wants to help me become a mature Christian. He doesn't want me to fail over and over again. He will cause me to grow—one way or another.

This is a fallen world and I am a fallen creature. I can't expect perfection in myself because only God is perfect. God never intended life on earth to be perfect. Yet He continues to work in my life.

In a doorway at home we have marks measuring the growth of our four sons from childhood to adulthood. Because I saw our sons daily, I didn't see their short-range growth. Yet in the long range, they have grown up to be handsome, tall young men. I could have started fretting that they weren't growing, but in time I could see them progressing.

God has all the time in the world. He has never failed, and He is not going to begin failing with me. Many of today's models, whether of the Christian life or marriage or child rearing, are overly idealistic. I'll only start fretting if I take them too seriously.

God expects steady, often imperceptible growth within me day after day, year after year, from the moment of my spiritual birth until the moment I step into His presence. He's holding me and has no intention of dropping me. Romans 8:29 says that His goal is to conform me to the image of His Son. The Bible's most precious promises deal with the absolute certainty that God is going to do what He says He will do. And He will persevere with me—to the end.

. . . he who began a good work in you will carry it on to completion until the day of Christ Jesus.

Philippians 1:6b

Why Fret The Clutch?

KURT C. WARD

One of my co-workers decided it was time for a new car. His indulgence? A fire-engine red, 16 valve, 4.6 liter, five-speed, racing convertible. You know the kind; it accelerates from zero to Mach 1 in 2.4 seconds, has a trunk big enough for one videotape, and the mechanical roar of a charging rhinoceros. There was only one problem: he had never driven a car with a clutch.

Once underway, he drives with the best. The problem is he can't get going. When stopped at a light, or on the slightest incline, his heart palpitates in time with his idling engine. The sweat on his forehead forms drops the size of quarters. He frets over stalling. He frets over horns honking. He frets he'll roll back or lurch straight into traffic. He has all the power he needs, if he'll just let out the clutch and step on the gas.

I do the same thing when God prompts me to take action. I may need to start from a standstill. I may need to upshift or downshift. There will be hills and steep grades, but like my friend, I'm afraid to take my foot off the clutch and step on the gas. I fret stalling out from fear, rolling back in sin, the honking horns of hecklers, and the jeers from disgruntled detractors. I fret over falling, and I fret over failing. I fret about how I'll look, rather than what I might accomplish. Yet, I have all the power I need.

All God requires is that I move into gear. I know how to drive; I just need some direction. He'll have plenty of mileposts and road signs along the way. He'll let me know where to turn, when to stop, and when to change lanes. All I need to do is let out the clutch, and release the old attitudes and actions that hold me in place. All I need to do is step on the gas, and engage the gears of Biblical principles and promises that sustain my momentum. And it's as simple as letting God tell me what to say, where to go, and how to act.

Then I heard the voice of the Lord saying, "Whom shall I send? And who will go for us?" And I said, "Here am I. Send me!"

Isaiah 6:8

Why Fret Comparing Trash?

KAREN POLAND

I had to laugh at myself this morning as I carried my three bags of garbage out to the curb for pickup. I actually caught myself thinking, "Why is it that I always have more trash than my neighbors?" You see, God has been showing me lately my tendency to compare myself to others. It amused me that I would fret even about my trash. It's not like the city is offering a prize for the household with the least trash!

Now, I seriously doubt that having more trash on my curb than my neighbors will affect my self-esteem or stunt my spiritual growth. However, when I give into this urge to compare my life to others, it can take its toll.

Think about your own life. How much stress and frustration are you adding because of a tendency to compare yourself to others? Do you look at a friend's spiritual gifts and conclude that you can never measure up to them? Do you compare your quiet, reserved spouse to another that is more outgoing and friendly? Perhaps your temptation is to fret about material possessions, or styles of parenting, or how/when you practice your spiritual disciplines. The possibilities are endless.

Oftentimes when we compare ourselves with others, we tend to compare one person's strength to another person's weakness. This can cause one of two things to occur. Either we see ourselves as less than we should, or we see ourselves greater than we should. Whichever we choose, comparisons rarely give us an accurate and true picture. It will either cause us to have pride or cause us to feel defeated.

The truth is that we all have areas of strength and areas of weakness. We all have gifts and talents that are unique. This is all part of God's design and purpose for the body of Christ. God does not desire that we fret over what we are not, but that we offer to Him all that we are. Rejoice then, in the person He has made you to be. Glorify Him in all that you are. And take those tendencies to compare out with the trash!

We do not dare to classify or compare ourselves with some who commend themselves. When they measure themselves by themselves and compare themselves with themselves, they are not wise.

2 Corinthians 10:12

Why Fret Dragons?

LINDA SHEPHERD

Five-year-old Jimmy had been spending the evening in his handicapped sister's room. After whispering secrets into her ear, he gave her a big kiss on the cheek, then moved to the desk to draw her a few pictures.

His re-occurring theme seemed to be great fire-breathing dragons scorching spiders.

When he was through, he looked up at nurse Sharon. "I'm going to leave these in here for Laura, tonight," he said.

"That would be nice," Sharon said.

Jimmy's face clouded as he sifted through his winged-dragon drawings. "I just hope these pictures stay on the paper and don't turn real before morning."

I laughed when Sharon repeated the story to me. "You know," I commented, "maybe that kid's on to something. These dragon drawings are a lot like our worries."

"Why do you say that?" Sharon asked with a mischievous grin.

"How often do we paint worries in our minds, then hope they don't become real?"

Sharon laughed. "Too often, I guess."

But, I wondered later, *what should we do with our mind-imagined dragons? How can we slay what isn't real?*

As I've thought about this dilemma, I've come to realize I'm not in control of my life in the first place. The best thing I can do is to give the control *I never had* to God. When I do, I'm not afraid of the dragons I paint in my times of fretting. Even if they *do* come to life, I have a God Whom I can trust to see me through.

What a relief it is to rely on Him, instead of myself, to slay my dragons. After all, His care is really the safest place to be.

For he is our God and we are the people of his pasture, the flock under his care.

Psalm 95:7a

Why Fret Creativity?

LYNN MORRISSEY

With Bible School fast-approaching, I grew increasingly intimidated. How could I ever relate to five-year-olds? With God's help, and that of snacks, crafts, and naps, I survived and so did the kids. This was fun!

My euphoria was short-lived when the next day chaos erupted. A girl's cries competed with a teacher's escalating scoldings. "No, no," she insisted, "You can't mix the Play-Doh®. What a mess! We can't separate the colors." It seemed like much ado over nothing. Suppressing a sob, the child dutifully returned unused doh lumps to corresponding colored cans.

I asked the lead teacher, Sandy, why we couldn't mix the colors. She thoughtfully replied, "No one ever has."

Then grinning mischievously, she added, "But I don't see why we couldn't!"

The next day Play-Doh® cans stood sentinel, their contents ready for transformation within small, hot palms. The children stoically fashioned monochromatic animals—tigers barely distinguishable from leopards, horses from zebras.

Challenging the children's complacency, I dared they mix the colors. Reticently they blended similar hues. With gradual daring, then Van Gogh abandon, they juxtaposed vibrant tints creating a smorgasbord of color.

"Teacher! Teacher! How 'bout a tomato pizza?" "See my rainbow!" "What about my tiger lilies?" "Here's a butterfly! I stuck my caterpillar in the can."

With a little coaxing, lackluster doh lumps transformed into kaleidoscopic creations. Creative children emerged like butterflies.

How often had I suffered "monochromania," fretting over whether or not to mix my colors, choosing conformity over creativity, fearing man's censure for breaking man's rules, and refusing bold risks for God?

How often had I inflicted "monochromania" on others by fretting over their actions, thus relegating them to "newsprint" existence and discouraging a display of their creative colors in Christ? I subjected them to guilt when they didn't conform to my "religious rules."

God, law-giver and judge, provides non-negotiable commandments to protect us. They're black and white with no indistinguishable gray shades. We should obey them.

God is also One of love and grace, the creator of colorful rainbows and colorful people, Who bestows unique gifts and callings. Who am I to prescribe "conformity commands" for God's creative children and stuff them like caterpillars into pre-labeled cocoons? Like our grace-giving Creator, instead I'll encourage His butterflies to spread their wings and fly!

Do not conform any longer to the pattern of this world, but be transformed by the renewing of your mind. Then you will be able to test and approve what God's will is— his good, pleasing and perfect will.

Romans 12:2

Why Fret Being Corrected?

CORA LEE PLESS

It was time for my children to be in the car and on their way to school when my eight-year-old son suddenly exclaimed, "Mom, you've got to check my math!"

"What do you mean?" I asked. "You didn't tell me I was supposed to check your homework."

I grabbed the calculator. Fourteen problems shouldn't take long.

"And there better not be any wrong!" Chip added emphatically.

However, two were incorrect. I dared to show them to Chip. As usual, he hated admitting his mistakes. He stood with tears streaming down his face and scolded me, as though it were my fault the answers were wrong.

"You can correct them on the way to school," I said, trying to calm him as I hurried him out the door.

Chip had wanted me to check the problems because his teacher required it, but he didn't want me to inform him of the ones that were wrong. What was the point in checking the problems if I couldn't show him the mistakes?

Several days later I sat silently in church during a service that focused on private confession. At first I thought, "I can't think of anything I need to confess." Yet as I quietly waited before God, I remembered times I had lost my temper with the children. Times I had acted selfishly. Times I had replaced trust in God with worry.

I began to recognize mistakes I needed to acknowledge, sins that called for repentance. Perhaps my greatest mistake was thinking I had nothing to confess.

Often I come to God as my son came to me. I ask God to examine my life; but I really don't want to be shown my mistakes. I don't like to admit my imperfections.

I'm learning that I don't have to fret about being perfect. That quality belongs only to God. God loves me even when I fail. Once I recognize that, I can allow God to correct me and show me my sins. Then I can rely on Him to help me grow toward maturity in His grace.

Search me, O God, and know my heart; test me and know my anxious thoughts. See if there is any offensive way in me, and lead me in the way everlasting.

Psalm 139:23–24

Why Fret Getting Credit?

ROBERT SCHULLER

God can do tremendous things through the person who doesn't care who gets the credit. Years ago, I met a man who was president and chairman of the board of a company in Minneapolis. The company had made the first huge balloon satellite, one that moved across the night sky like a star. It was a successful step in the early stages of the space program. I said to the president, "Excuse me for saying this, but I've never heard of your name or your company."

He replied, "Maybe not. We didn't get the credit, but we got the contract."

Don't worry about getting the credit. If you do, you'll become ego-involved in the decision-making moments of life. Decisions must never be based on ego needs. They must be based on human needs and market pressures that transcend your own desires. Decide today: Would you rather satisfy your ego—or enjoy the fruit of success?

O LORD, you are my God; I will exalt you and praise your name, for in perfect faithfulness you have done marvelous things, things planned long ago.

Isaiah 25:1

(Pages 107–108, *Tough Times Never Last, But Tough People Do!* Robert H. Schuller, Crystal Cathedral Ministries, 1983. Used by permission.)

Why Fret Pleasure In Work?

H. NORMAN WRIGHT

What part does work play in your life? Perhaps these questions can help you evaluate the place of work in your life.

Do you spend a lot of time thinking about the satisfaction you're receiving from your job, or what you wish would happen?

In what way is your job furthering the kingdom of God here on earth? If your job were taken away from you for the next six months how would you feel about yourself?

If someone asked you to explain how you experience God's pleasure in your work, what would you say?

Remember Eric Liddell in the Oscar-winning movie, *Chariots of Fire?* Everything Liddell did was for the glory of God. His sister felt he was neglecting his calling as a missionary to China, and one day she was upset with him because he missed a missions meeting. Eric said to her, "Jennie, you've got to understand. I believe God made me for a purpose—for China. But he also made me fast! And when I run, I feel his pleasure."

Can you say that about what you do?

And whatever you do, whether in word or deed, do it all in the name of the Lord Jesus, giving thanks to God the Father through him.

Colossians 3:17

(Page 24, *Promises and Priorities*, H. Norman Wright, Vine Books, MI, 1997)

Why Fret Bad Days?

SHIRLEY POPE WAITE

A popular children's book tells of a boy who had a horrible, terrible, bad day. During the children's sermon, the pastor asked the boys and girls if they'd ever had that kind of day. They nodded their heads in agreement.

He then explained, "Endorphins are natural hormone-like substances with painkilling and tranquilizing properties, secreted by the brain. They magnify our feelings in ninety seconds.

"So, when you're going through a bad time, just say, 'Endorphins, you *can't* make me have a bad day! I'm going to laugh so I can rejoice in the Lord!'"

All of us at times think, "But I have nothing to laugh about. My life is filled with terrible, horrible, bad days."

Try scheduling a ten-minute "humor" break every day. Maintain a humor "first-aid" kit. Stock it with cartoons, jokes, funny greeting cards, comedy tapes.

Too simplistic, you say? Play with a child and rediscover a sense of delight. Dare to be "silly" with the child.

If you're still not convinced, consider this. Some hospitals now maintain a humor "lab," a cheerful, brightly-lit room devoid of medical equipment. Instead, it is stocked with cassettes of classic radio shows featuring Abbott and Costello, Amos and Andy, as well as Candid Camera TV shows. Video tapes of Laurel and Hardy, W.C. Fields, Charlie Chaplin, Bob Hope specials, and other comedy shows are available. Joke and cartoon books lie around.

Yes, laughter is good for one's emotional and physical health. Chances are it will squelch that fretting, stress, and frustration when it rears its ugly head and tries to overwhelm you.

A cheerful heart is good medicine, but a crushed spirit dries up the bones.

Proverbs 17:22

Why Fret Nursery Leadership?

LORI WALL

"Sorry, kids. We've got to go to first service, 'cause I've got to work in the nursery again."

I felt let down after speaking with a volunteer who had called in sick. *It's too late to call someone else, which means I have to do it,* I muttered to myself. On this particular weekend, I'd hoped to sleep in and just go to our church's second service.

My daughter moaned, "Why don't you just quit?"

During my time as leader, I had tried to turn my position over to someone else but God had other plans.

When I first took over managing the church nursery, I lost people because they moved on to other ministries or needed to quit. I quickly learned I couldn't do it all myself. I cried out to the Lord for workers because I didn't want to burn out.

Before I knew it, the Lord began providing volunteers. There were even enough for some to be available "on call." Running the nursery went smoothly.

But then I went through another cycle of losing people, forcing me to be in the nursery more. I again became anxious, fretting about where I would get workers. I realized I needed to guard my tongue so that I didn't communicate to the parents that I didn't want to care for their babies. Again, the Lord showed His faithfulness and brought volunteers.

Now I'm striving to correct my thinking. The Lord is showing me that the times I work in the nursery are not only an opportunity to minister to the babies but to others as well: a volunteer, a parent, or even a teen coming in to hang out.

I am surrendering to the idea I will be nursery manager for awhile. When it's time for me to stop, the Lord will supply someone else to step in just as He has provided workers.

You were taught, with regard to your former way of life, to put off your old self, which is being corrupted by its deceitful desires; to be made new in the attitude of your minds; and to put on the new self, created to be like God in true righteousness and holiness.

Ephesians 4:22–24

Why Fret Needing Help?

SHERRI SHAFFER

What more could I want? I had a loving husband, two beautiful and healthy toddlers, a new home and the privilege of being a full time homemaker. I also had dishes piled in the sink, toys all over the floor, nothing prepared for dinner and my husband complaining he had no clean underwear!

Frustrated and guilty, I questioned my self worth. I had chosen to be a wife, mother and homemaker, but I wasn't very good at it! I was even raising my voice at my small children, something I thought I'd never do. I needed help!

It was at this time that I attended my first Bible study. The lesson was on the second chapter of John. Jesus attended a wedding and came to the rescue of the host family who had run out of wine. Jewish wedding feasts lasted a week and the groom was expected to have adequate provisions. Running out of food or wine was a social disgrace. Jesus changed water into wine and the host was praised for saving the best wine for last.

After reading this story, I had a revelation that changed my life. Jesus' first miracle was not a life and death situation and it wasn't an earth shaking event. Jesus' very first miracle was simply meeting a family's need and saving them from embarrassment! I always believed in God, but thought He was distant, sitting in heaven ruling the world at large. This Bible story showed me that God was a personal God who cared about my personal problems. I thought, "I don't have to do this all by myself. Jesus wants to help me get organized, plan meals and patiently care for my family!"

This was a whole new concept for me. That day I got on my knees and prayed, "Jesus, please come into my life and help me be the person I want to be."

A huge weight lifted off my shoulders when I realized that God not only cared about my everyday life and problems, He was there to give me practical help and solutions. He didn't want me to fret! There will always be stressful situations and challenges in this life, but now I know where to go for strength and guidance!

And I will ask the Father, and he will give you another Counselor to be with you forever.

John 14:16

Why Fret Big Steps?

MARY BETH NELSON

I enjoy working in my yard, but I must admit there are occasional annoyances. My electric lawnmower cord sometimes becomes entangled. Other times, after neatly stacking limbs against a fence, I find I need something that is lodged between the limbs and fence. When this happens, I quickly grab as many limbs as possible which accomplishes nothing except frustration and a few scratches to my arm.

If the idea of taking things "one step" or "one day at a time" is advantageous during life's major conflicts (and it is), why not apply it to the daily insignificant ones?

It is amazing how easily I reached the object by the fence when I decided to remove just "one limb at a time." When I began to untangle the lawnmower cord with just "one twist at a time," instead of my usual fretful yank, a surprising calmness replaced my anxiety.

During this welcome turn of events, I thought of how I allow my impatience to create unnecessary frustrations. God expects me to handle daily struggles, regardless of their trivialities, in an intelligent way pleasing to Him. He assures me that He's in control of both the big and small stuff, so why fret it?

What a serene life He offers if I will only take time to look for, acknowledge, and accept it!

The end of a matter is better than its beginning, and patience is better than pride. Do not be quickly provoked in your spirit, for anger resides in the lap of fools.

Ecclesiastes 7:8–9

Why Fret Speaking In Church?

IRENE CARLONI

Last Sunday in church, Fran gave a very moving testimony. It was exciting, uplifting and affected each of us. I noticed how comfortable she was when she was speaking to the congregation.

Why can't I be relaxed and have it all together when I speak to a large group of people? I fretted. *I get so tongue tied and bashful. I get too many ideas in my head of what I want to say. I try to sort them out, but I end up saying three different things at once. I have no problem facilitating a weekly Bible Study, so why do I get nervous when facing a larger group?*

When I made my daily phone call to my daughter, I poured out my heart to her about my anxiety and frustration. Her reply was quite an eye-opener for me.

"Mom, when Fran spoke, the Holy Spirit was leading her. When you let the Holy Spirit work through you, you will speak with the same conviction and excitement. It won't matter if it's a large group or a small group, you'll know exactly what to say. Don't get yourself upset over this. Have faith."

My attitude changed immediately. I closed the door on the anxiety and discouragement that I had allowed to enter my heart. Instead, I should have turned to the Lord first and brought my fears to Him. Fretting only kept me focused on myself, rather than God's abilities within me.

So we say with confidence, "The Lord is my helper; I will not be afraid . . ."

Hebrews 13:6

Why Fret
Retirement Activities?

ELAINE F. NAVARRO

When my husband and I retired six years ago, it was like beginning a new life. We moved from a large city to a small beach community. After the initial settling down to retirement living, I decided to fulfill some promises made earlier of becoming more involved in my church and our community.

The difficulty, I soon found out, was deciding which undertakings to pursue. Prison ministry? Visiting the sick? Feeding the hungry? There were so many. The first year I settled on cooking for the homeless once a month, weekly phoning for prayer meetings and Bible Study every Thursday. As for community obligations, I stepped up my long time habit of writing opinions to the local daily newspaper. I even picketed a county board of supervisors' meeting to protest extending the life of a landfill that polluted nearby neighborhoods. Yet, every time I heard a request from the pulpit or read a newspaper, I still felt an overwhelming guilt if I didn't sign up to help elsewhere.

Earlier years had been jammed full of family obligations and, in more recent years, full time employment. I saw myself growing older. Yet, at a time when I should be slowing down a bit, I felt a strong urging to give even more of myself. Trying to juggle it all made my soul feel fretful and depressed.

While praying over this dilemma, everything I read seemed to say relax, leave everything to God. It was then I knew that I was fretting too much. Instead of being a team player I was trying to be the team captain, which is God's job. That realization leveled off personal expectations.

No longer do I try to do it all. I moderately volunteer these days, asking the Lord to guide me in His direction. I also take time to relax and enjoy life. A favorite treat is train travel and I even wrote a poem about riding the Amtrak.

Ah! Life is good without fretting!

He makes me lie down in green pastures, he leads me beside quiet waters, he restores my soul. He guides me in paths of righteousness for his name's sake.

Psalm 23:2–3

Why Fret
A Voice "Warble"?

NORA LACIE ABELL

My face still prickles with the memory. After auditioning for a talent show with a musical number, a tactless schoolmate asked: "Why do you do that warble-thing with your voice?" Her words slapped me on the cheek and as I struggled for an answer, my sense of worth took a dive downward.

Years later, under the teaching of an experienced voice coach, I discovered that this particular "warble," or vibrato, is a desirable, natural quality, but the shame I experienced at that innocently ignorant remark kept me from singing in public for twenty years. I wished then I could remove it from my throat.

Is there something you would remove from yourself? Of course there is! That's human nature! My very Swedish-looking daughter wishes she "could be more Native-American." I always admired the straight and shiny hair of the Asian girls, mine being unruly and frizzy. We fret and compare ourselves to others who may be thinner, blonder, darker, have smaller feet or fatter bankrolls. We admire fewer freckles and someone else's sense of humor, poise, musical ability, fitness level or scientific mind. We spend enormous amounts of energy worrying about what we *are not,* forgetting what we were created *to be.*

Did God mess up? Doesn't He know I "should" be taller? He knows exactly how smart, athletic and artistic (and tall) we should be! He designed each human to embody qualities unique to that person, distinct and lovely, so that we wouldn't look like cookie-cutter designs.

We have a part in this, too. We need to recognize and rejoice in our own custom-designed set of features and traits, as well as begin to see our parents and children within a whole new frame of acceptance. Friends, co-workers, schoolmates, and neighbors possess the same "mark of excellence" as we do, and it's a lot of fun identifying their special qualities.

This doesn't mean we behave as if we don't care about developing our talents or taking care of our health and appearance. But it removes our fretting and puts it back in the hands of the Master Designer where it belongs! Instead of redesigning ourselves in an image we think becomes us more handsomely, we can seek to celebrate those winning features in others, as well as ourselves. Let yourself "warble!"

I praise you because I am fearfully and wonderfully made; your works are wonderful I know that full well.

Psalm 139:14

Why Fret A New Table?

C. ELLEN WATTS

The moment my friend, Amy, saw the table in the furniture store's window, she wanted it. Since her husband, Dwight's, work car had to be held together with daily prayer, she vowed to keep mum concerning the table.

Two hours later, as her family of seven crowded around the rickety table with which she and Dwight had started housekeeping, the leaf beneath Dwight's dinner collapsed. So did her vow.

After first looking at the table (along with its price tag), Amy and Dwight shopped elsewhere for tables, mostly at yard sales. None would do. So Dwight gave her the table for Christmas and said, "It's a gift."

Enjoying the new feeling of not having to concern herself with payments, Amy gave full attention to its weekly polishing and fretted about keeping it perfect. She became adept at standing guard:

"Don't drop your books like that!"

"No! You may not use Play Doh® on Mamma's new table."

"Move that sandwich this minute!"

More often than not, she sent the children out to dine on the back steps.

"I thought we needed the larger table so we could all fit around it," Dwight commented.

"We do, but they spill so—"

Dwight sighed. "Sometimes I wonder if God meant for us to have that table or if I only imagined it."

"If God gave it to us, then the least I can do is to keep it nice!" Amy snapped.

Then one evening Amy's friend Carol brought her daughter over to work with Julie on a school project.

"May we paint on the table, Mom?" Julie asked.

Not wanting to ruin her Great Mom image before Carol, Amy reluctantly gave permission and instructed Julie to spread newspapers. Five minutes later, Julie's "Oh, no!" catapulted her to the dining room. Fear darkened Julie's eyes as she backed against the wall clutching a dripping paint can. Amy glared at her, fists clenched. She had spread newspapers all right, but not nearly far enough.

Suddenly, Amy felt a strong, warm hand covering her own and heard Carol pray softly, "Lord, you know this child is worth more than a thousand tables . . ."

In that moment, Amy realized she had been fretting about something destined to be destroyed. Only people would live forever. The children were hers to care for and "polish." The table and other possessions were but gifts from God to assist with rearing.

Lest Amy ever forgot the lesson of that day, a trace of orange remains on the table to remind her. It's a reminder to me, too, each time I visit her.

Live as children of light . . . and find out what pleases the Lord.

Ephesians 5: 8,10

Why Fret Stolen Jewelry?

PENNY PIERCE ROSE

For my fortieth birthday, my mother was working hard to come up with the perfect gift for me. One day she called and said, "I've decided to take some of my old jewelry and have it remade into a diamond necklace for your birthday!" Who could say no to that?

We began looking for the perfect setting and researching where to take the jewelry to have it reset. Not long after, I received another phone call from my mom. Her voice was no longer excited, but devastated, "Someone's stolen all my nice jewelry, including the things I meant for you to have."

After consoling my mother and reminding her that the jewelry didn't mean nearly as much to me as she did, I hung up the phone and began to think about the treasures I do have; the ones which cannot be taken away. By remembering the treasures I have in God, I was able to get past the pain of losing the elusive treasures that had been snatched away before they reached my neck.

I realized that, like my earthly mother, I have a Heavenly Father who wants to give me good gifts. While He has blessed me with material things, He has also blessed me with other precious treasures. When I see the beauty of a New Mexico sunset, I am in awe of the gift of creation. When I hear the cry of a newborn baby, I find myself praising Him for the gift of life. When I read a passage of Scripture which changes my heart, I marvel at His supernatural ability to speak to me personally through a book written centuries before I was born. Watching people go forward at an altar call brings me to tears as I remember the gift of salvation so freely given to me.

The experience of the stolen jewelry revealed to me the importance of being thankful for the many gifts God has bestowed upon me. Won't you take the time to thank Him for the treasures He has given to you?

Therefore, since we are receiving a kingdom that cannot be shaken, let us be thankful, and so worship God acceptably with reverence and awe.

Hebrews 12:28

Why Fret Short-Sightedness?

PAMELA F. DOWD

Living near the woods, I am often amazed at what God teaches me on my daily walks. Once, when feeling discouraged, God energized me. I had been singing, "As the deer panteth for the water, so my soul longeth after Thee." When I came upon a deer standing in my path, my heart soared.

The other day I had several important decisions making me fret. I needed a break, so I went out for a walk. I came upon several neighbors eating wild plums. After asking where they had found them, I set out looking for the tree myself. When I came to the little fruit tree, I felt disappointed. They had explained that the ripe plums were yellow, but most of the plums I saw were green. I guessed they had stripped the tree of all its mature fruit. I gathered the one or two small plums still left, then looked on the ground. Several had fallen free, and feeling like Ruth, I gleaned the ripe plums, inspecting each one for wormholes and bird peckings. Then I took my little handful and thanked God.

As a writer, I'm rarely without a book in hand, even when walking. So, after consuming the bittersweet plums, I continued reading and walking. I made the three-mile journey around the lake, and when I returned to the little tree I looked up from my book, and thanked God again. There, to my surprise, stood a large plum tree filled with ripe fruit directly next to the original little tree. The answer to my decision became clear. It wasn't that this tree was hidden from my sight when I first stopped, it was that I was so busy concentrating on what was in front of me that I failed to look farther ahead.

As I walked home, I forgot about my book and thought about life. How often do I fret about the limitations right in front of me that I forget to raise my vision to the possibilities all around me? When life presents me with the most obvious choice, do I take it readily, often missing the bigger blessing? Instead, I want to embrace each challenge with grace and anticipation.

Now to him who is able to do immeasurably more than all we ask or imagine, . . . to him be glory . . .

Ephesians 3:20–21

Why Fret Weight?

PAMELA F. DOWD

I carried thirty extra pounds for ten years. While overweight, I tried every kind of diet. I walked three miles, five times a week and worked out on Nautilus equipment. Still the weight remained.

I moaned to the doctor. He checked my thyroid to no avail. I complained to my friends and family. They offered no help other than to tell me I didn't look horrible. Ha! I felt bad and knew I looked terrible. I could see it in pictures. I became obsessed with the scales; I weighed every morning.

One day I decided I'd had enough. I had a conversation with God that went something like this, "God, You made me. You formed me in my mother's womb. Before anything was created, You knew what I would become. You made me for a purpose. In Your Word, You tell me that I am not to worry about what to wear or eat. Well, God, I worry about clothing because I look awful. I worry about eating because all I think about is what I can and what I can't put in my mouth.

"I confess, Lord, I'm obsessed with my weight. I have not turned it over to You and walked away. I have tried everything. I have no peace. Help me! I believe You created me for a better purpose than this foolishness. I believe You can control my weight even though I can't. I'm going to quit fretting and give this to You. Teach me when to eat and what to eat. Make my exercise effective. I will not worry about my weight anymore; I give it to You. I will do whatever You tell me. Fill me with Your Spirit and give me the self-control You promise. In Jesus name, Amen."

I prayed that prayer two years ago. Now I weigh thirty pounds less. Taking off the weight took discipline, but God taught me how to eat right and exercise effectively. He taught me tricks for weight loss, but most of all He taught me to trust Him.

Today I am healthy, slim and happy. I found peace because I trusted the Creator instead of fretting about how I looked.

. . . do not worry about your life, what you will eat or drink; or about your body . . .

Matthew 6:25

Why Fret Asking Why?

SHANNON WOODWARD

Sometime around my son's seventh birthday, a change came over our household. Zac turned from compliant, trusting child into . . . "The Questioner." I went from wise, all-knowing mother to . . . "The Suspect."

"Dinner's at five," I'd announce.

The Questioner would eye me with suspicion. "Why five? We usually eat at six."

I'd go shopping and buy apples. He'd wonder aloud why I didn't buy oranges.

Almost overnight, the tone of his questions took on a "bare-light-bulb-hanging-over-hard-chair" feel. "Why did you park on this side of the parking lot?" began to sound a lot like "Where were you on the night of June third?"

Finally I asked myself a question: "Why do I put up with all this?"

I knew something would have to change if we were both to survive. So I learned a new phrase—one I had vowed never to use, but which soon became the foundation of all our discussions: "Because I'm the mother."

I liked everything about that phrase. It was powerful. It was effective. For a time, it was all I said. In the end, though, I decided to reserve it for the truly desperate moments.

In His own way, God says those same words to us. Just ask Job. He wanted an explanation for his suffering. God's answer? "Where were you when I laid the earth's foundation . . . shut up the sea behind doors . . . made the clouds its garment? . . . Will the one who contends with the Almighty correct Him?"

Translation: "Because I'm God."

Job's answer was rightfully humble. "Surely I spoke of things I did not understand. . . . "

Translation: "I'm not God. I'll try to remember that."

Once, after a full day of defending myself, I said to Zac, "When I say no, it would be nice if you just said, 'Yes, Ma'am'."

Zac was quiet for a moment, then nodded. "I bet that would be a nice treat for you, huh Mom?"

Maybe God would like a nice treat occasionally. Maybe instead of me questioning His every move in my life, He'd like me to express my absolute trust in His wisdom, sovereignty and love. Maybe He'd like me to just say, "Yes, Sir," once in awhile.

I'll try not to question so much. Except I do need to ask one last, nagging question. I just have to know, "Lord, why on earth do You put up with me?"

Then Job replied to the LORD: "I know that you can do all things; no plan of yours can be thwarted."

Job 42:1–2

Why Fret Unpleasant Feelings?

JAN JOHNSON

Each week it got worse. As I traveled back and forth to work in a car pool, I thought I would explode. It seemed to me that one of my coworkers and car-pool companions complained nonstop. I tried to pray for her, but I am not the saint I would like to be. At traffic signals, I wanted to bolt from the van and run.

I considered that she was emotionally needy and I admitted to God that I could not make her okay—nor was I willing to try. When I prayed for her, I imagined her sitting in God's lap, which is an image I often use for myself when I feel needy. This helped for a while, but by the next week, I still wanted to flee the van.

While digging around in our storage shed, I discovered a child-size rocking chair that had been my daughter's. I tilted it and watched it rock. A spontaneous prayer for my coworker occurred somewhere within me. *Hhhm, interesting.* I dragged the rocking chair into my kitchen and placed it in a corner. It was in the way and didn't fit my kitchen's contemporary look, but it helped. Each time I walked by it, I tilted it and offered a breath prayer for my coworker. I can't report that I became instantly patient with her, because I didn't. But the resentment was gone, and I guessed that

God was pleased with that much obedience. And more of my life was filled with an awareness of God's companionship.

Some of us seem afraid to tell God about the anger and frustration that He already knows we feel. Or we deny feeling anger because we assume that God and anger cannot coexist. Instead, we put on a "looking good, kid" image with God—we look good, we feel good, we are good. Anger and frustration are regarded as obstacles to be overcome and replaced with worthy feelings—before we talk to God.

To abide in God's presence means that we don't have to dress up our feelings. If we believe God is grand enough to love our flawed self, we can speak the truth to Him about what we feel.

In your anger do not sin: Do not let the sun go down while you are still angry, and do not give the devil a foothold.

Ephesians 4:26–27

(Pages 54–56, adapted from *Enjoying the Presence of God*, Jan Johnson, NavPress, 1996. Used by permission.)

Why Fret Busyness?

PAMELA GRUBBE

Finally! Saturday arrived. I'd had a busy week with clients fretting over every suggestion I made. On top of today's list was time with God. I looked forward to the peace and quiet.

As the television shouted from the living room and a Star Wars game battled on the computer in the den, I grabbed my Bible and headed for the peacefulness of the backyard.

Settling down on a chaise lounge, I began to read. Suddenly wings flapped over me; birds were calling and screeching as they fought over food at the feeding station. I knew by their call they were Steller Jays, one of my favorites.

Stellers (Cyanocitta stelleri) are larger than a robin, mostly blue in color with the crest and foreparts black. In the family of crows and magpies, jays are especially intelligent. When not raiding campgrounds, their diet consists of grain, nuts and insects. Helpful to trees, these birds also fatten themselves and their young on tree-attacking beetles and insects. Though quiet and sensitive near the nest, Stellers are noisy and seem to enjoy causing loud disturbances. Their calls vary from rowdy to raucous, so they generally do not go unnoticed.

In our daily lives, we find ourselves bombarded with a noisy, fretful world. The demands of schedule, problems, and tomorrow's uncertainties can weigh heavily. Many people in the Bible, including Jesus, withdrew at times from their busy worlds to quiet themselves and pray. Learning from the Stellar, who is quiet near its nest, may we know when to silence ourselves and listen to God.

William A. Ward said, "Skillful listening is the best remedy for loneliness, loquaciousness, and laryngitis."

But Jesus often withdrew to lonely places and prayed.

Luke 5:16

Why Fret Consistent Prayer?

RENIE PARSONS

Several years ago, my prayer life was interrupted by a baby. I no longer washed the dishes in peace and quiet. It got harder and harder to find time to talk to God.

Strangely enough, my dental hygienist gave me the answer. Don't you just hate it when she asks if you floss? I always hem and haw and clear my throat and finally say, "No...but, I know that I should." And, then, traditionally, comes the "Importance of Flossing" speech. But this hygienist was different. Really different.

She said, "Don't worry about flossing every day. It just doesn't work for some people to make this a morning or evening ritual."

I was thrilled! Permission to skip flossing. Ah, the freedom of it!

Then she asked, "Can I just make one suggestion? Just floss whenever you think about it."

Fine. No problem. That was do-able. I could manage to floss just when I thought about it. I left the office that day feeling great.

But, you know what? I think of flossing almost every day. So, I floss almost every day. Not perfectly. Not every day, including holidays and vacations. Just when I think about it.

I decided that could apply to prayer, too. So, now, I just pray every time I think about it. I'm not a morning person, but by the time I'm dressed and get everyone out the door, I have a few minutes to myself. I frequently spend that time in prayer. I also listen to a set of tapes of the New Testament. It's uplifting and encouraging. I try to pick a tape that coordinates with whatever Bible study or class I'm participating in at the time.

I've also found out there are some things I want to pray about every time I think about them . . . like my two daughters. Every day I thank God for them. I ask God to watch over them and keep them safe. Sometimes I throw in a request or two, but mostly, I just keep them before God. I also pray for my husband every time I think about him, thanking God for the blessing he is in my life.

On any given day, someone I know is having a crisis. Sometimes great. Sometimes small. But every time I think about him or her, I pray. Just a brief message to God to let that person see His will and continue to follow Him—or find Him.

That's my guilt-free philosophy of quiet time. You have to snatch it wherever and whenever you can. God is always available. You can't call too early. You can't call too late. Just don't forget to call. That way you won't fret about prayer.

The LORD is righteous in all his ways and loving toward all he has made. The LORD is near to all who call on him, to all who call on him in truth. He fulfills the desires of those who fear him; he hears their cry and saves them.

Psalm 145:17–19

Why Fret $260?

SHANNON WOODWARD

"What should we do?" I asked my husband, panic edging my voice.

"Stop worrying. We'll be fine," Dave answered.

His calmness upset me. We needed $260 by the following day to pay for Dave's last quarter of college tuition, or else he couldn't register. Yet here he stood, unconcerned and unruffled. We'd never find the money with that attitude.

"How can you be so calm?"

He shrugged. "I prayed about it. God will provide."

"Praying's fine," I fretted in silence, "but what we really need here is some action."

I began digging through the closet, searching coat pockets and running my hands along the floor. I knew there was little chance I'd find $260 that way, but it felt good to try.

"By the way, your parents invited us over for dinner," Dave said.

The suggestion sounded good, although I knew it would be hard not to tell my parents about our dilemma. They'd gladly give us the money, but we'd already decided it was time we began fixing our own problems.

Dinner was great. Sitting there pretending not to have a care in the world, however, was difficult.

Just as we finished, my mother brought me a pile of mail she'd been saving. One letter was from a former employer, whom I hadn't worked for in two years. The first page was jumbled legal jargon. The second had a perforated check at the bottom, made out to me—for $262 dollars.

I don't recall buying or receiving stock options. I don't know why my employer decided at that time to cash me out, but it didn't matter. What I learned in that moment is that God is a master planner, able to see what lies ahead on my path and able to provide before I have an actual need.

We needed $260 and God provided. He even gave us a little extra so we could stop for coffee on the way home from the bank.

That's just the kind of Father He is. Why fret when He already knows how He's going to provide?

And my God will meet all your needs according to his glorious riches in Christ Jesus.

Philippians 4:19

Why Fret Removing Trees?

FLORENCE FERRIER

We had dreamed about spending the whole summer at our "up north" retreat. Then one summer we did just that—but only because Darwin had a heart attack during the first week of his vacation. Finally in late August, his local doctor released him to return to work. We took a leisurely walk around the yard and settled in the lawn chairs.

Suddenly Darwin declared he was going to take down three popple trees in our yard which hadn't leafed out that year. He hadn't enjoyed seeing them leafless all summer and wanted them gone!

This didn't seem like a project he was ready for; yet, I knew he was increasingly impatient with inactivity now that he felt better. Something stopped me from warning him about undoing his recovery. Instead I sent up a silent, desperate prayer. "Lord, You know he doesn't want to hear anything from me about this. If he shouldn't be doing this now, I need You to whisper in his ear. Please!"

Within a few minutes after he set to work, Darwin stopped for a breather. He rested for quite some time. Before going back into action, he said, "We'll just do this one tree now. This is too hard on a hot day."

My spirit almost zinged in a silent thanksgiving as I said, "I'm sure you're right . . . . "

That was the fastest, most specific answer to prayer I had ever witnessed! By resting three times, Darwin completed his scaled-down goal. Later in the day he used the car to drag the tree out of the yard, delegating me to rake up the debris.

That memory still serves me as an unforgettable private lesson in trusting. Why fret when I can trust? God *is* listening and He *is* able . . . although He doesn't necessarily answer all my prayers exactly as I'd like.

When I am afraid, I will trust in you.

Psalm 56:3

Why Fret Making Decisions?

EUNICE ANN BADGLEY

I have a hard time making decisions. Since I fret about all possible outcomes, I find myself getting frustrated and sometimes make no decision at all.

I wish I could handle things as easily as my four-year-old grandson. My daughter recently talked to him about the possibility of a job change. It would mean a move across the state to the area where I live. Jared looked up toward heaven and said, "God, do you want us to move close to my grandma?"

He continued to look up a moment, listening. Then he told his mother, "He said 'yes.' "

That kind of trust is what God deserves. Perhaps a four-year-old has a direct line to God because his life has not become cluttered with fretting about things. He simply looks up, asks a question and waits for an answer.

The answers don't always come as quickly and plainly as Jared thought his answer came, but his kind of faith is what God wants. Ask and trust Him to answer.

Ask the LORD for rain in the springtime; it is the LORD who makes the storm clouds. He gives showers of rain to men, and plants of the field to everyone.

Zechariah 10:1

Why Fret Little Foxes?

TINA KRAUSE

What makes you fume? You know, those bothersome little annoyances in life that create fretting? For instance:

You set the alarm one hour earlier than usual to ensure you have plenty of time to jog a few miles, read the morning newspaper, and drink a leisurely cup of coffee before dressing for work. But the alarm fails to wake you because your five-year-old accidentally pushed the button when he woke you up at 3 a.m. with a stomachache.

So instead of rising at 6:00, it's now 7:30 and you're due at the office by 8:00. Splashing cold water on your face, you run a comb through your hair while you frantically scramble through your closet for something to wear. Then you remember that the outfit you had in mind is still at the cleaners.

Hurriedly, you throw on just any old thing as you dash through the kitchen en route to the garage. Instead of a leisurely cup of hot coffee, you settle for a cold glass of orange juice as you make your way onto the open road.

Before long, a school bus pulls in front of you and stops every other block, delaying you even longer.

It's now 8:15. Fuming yet?

The Bible teaches that it is the "little foxes" in life that "ruin the vineyards" (Song of Solomon 2:15). The real joy-robbers aren't the big catastrophes, but the trivial, everyday annoyances in life. One or two consecutive "foxes" have been known to hurl the best of us into an all-out tailspin, ruining an otherwise perfect day.

God's antidote for this kind of fretting is quite simple. I call it "The Three P's to Slaying Pesky Little Foxes:" Prayer plus Praise equals Peace. When we commit our way to God in prayer and choose to praise Him regardless of our circumstances, we will experience His supernatural peace.

Praise the LORD, O my soul; all my inmost being, praise his holy name. Praise the LORD, O my soul, and forget not all his benefits.

Psalm 103:1–2

Contributors

Nora Lacie Abell thrives with her family and the pines on a tree farm on the Colville Confederated Tribe's Reservation in rural Ferry County. Contact: Long Rifle Ranch, Box 644, Inchelium, WA 99138. (509) 738-6245.

Marie A. Asner is a musician/workshop presenter/writer. Summer 1998, she presented a poetry workshop for the national convention of the American Guild of Organists. Contact: P.O. Box 4343, Overland Park, KS 66204-0343. FAX: (913) 385-5369.

Eunice Ann Badgley is a 58-year-old widow, mother, and grandmother. She graduated from Park College at age 53. She enjoys reading, writing, crafts, water aerobics, and her grandchildren. Contact: 451 Spring Ave, Liberty, MO 64068. (816) 781-8908.

Cindy Bailey writes features each week for the Pittsburgh/Greensburg *Tribune-Review*. Her Christian columns, crafts, and songs appear often in *Parent Life* and *Shining Star*. Contact: R.D. #1, box 191-B, Waynesburg, PA. (724) 852-2563. cinswind@greenepa.net.

Esther M. Bailey is a freelance writer with more than 600 published credits. She and her husband Ray frequently remind each other not to fret the God stuff. Contact: 4631 E. Solano Dr., Phoenix, AZ 85018. (602) 840-3143.

Vickey Banks is an inspirational speaker and writer with a passion to help others experience a dynamic and intimate walk with God. She is very happily married and the mother of two great kids. Contact: (405) 728-2305.

Ellen Bergh is a motivational speaker and writer. She facilitates the High Desert Christian Writers Guild where writers perfect their craft to glorify God, giver of all good things. Contact: 3600 Brabham Avenue, Rosamond, CA 93560. mastermedia@hughes.net.

C. Louise Brooks and her husband live in the Mojave desert in California. She is a retired USAF secretary, a mother of three girls, and a grandmother. Contact: 13311 Clement St. North, Edwards, CA 93623. (760) 769-4443.

Jan Brunette is the mother of four, the stepmother of seven, and the grandmother of twenty. Her articles appeared in *The Lutheran Witness*, *Resource*, *Baptist Leader*, and many other publications. Jan has taught in Christian schools for thirteen years. Contact: 2711 Bayview Drive, Eustis, FL 32726. (352) 357-7097. brunette@cde.com.

Kitty Bucholtz, president of Creative Copy Ink and Tempe Christian Writers Club, writes fiction, nonfiction and marketing materials, and edits a business magazine. Contact: PO Box 68114, Phoenix, AZ 85082-8114. jkbuch@primenet.com.

Charlotte H. Burkholder is a freelance writer holding a certificate of completion from the Christian Writer's Guild and has had a number of articles published. Contact: 2128 Eversole Rd, Harrisonburg, VA 22802. (540) 434-2907. marlincpa@aol.com

Penny Carlevato, RN, has three children and is founder/owner of "Penelope's Tea Time." She is a freelance writer, teaches at colleges, and speaks about sharing God's love through having afternoon tea. Contact: P.O. Box 2215, El Segundo, CA 90245. (310) 640-2190. teatime@eni.net.

Irene Carloni writes newsletters, devotionals, poems, lyrics, and is an editor and producer. She enjoys photography, crafts, and Bible study. The Carlonis have three children. Contact: 6 Cambridge, Manhatten Beach, CA 90266. Aicarloni@earthlink.net.

Libby C. Carpenter is a freelance writer and former educator. Previously published in *God's Abundance* and *God's Unexpected Blessings*, she desires to bless others through devotionals and short stories. Contact: 426 Aderholdt Rd, Lincolnton, NC 28092. libbyac2 @juno.com

Jeri Chrysong, a poet and humorist, resides in Huntington Beach, CA, with sons Luc and Sam, who drive her crazy. Jeri's work has been featured in newspapers, devotionals, and the *God's Vitamin "C" for the Spirit* series. She enjoys long walks on the beach.

Cathy Clark is married to her best friend, Duane Clark. Together they write songs, minister in music all over the world, and home school their two great kids, Nici and Jason. Contact: duaneclark@qnet.com

Glenna M. Clark and her husband Burt have been missionaries most of their fifty-two years of married life. They graduated from Biola in 1948 and have served the Lord in Jamaica, the Philippines, and Guatemala. Contact: 5200 E. Irvine Blvd. #380, Irvine, CA 92620. (714) 832-5434

Joan Clayton is the author of five books and over 350 published articles. She and her husband Emmitt reside in Portales, New Mexico. "Emmitt is God's gift to me," she says. "I am so blessed!"

Gayle Cloud is a credentialed teacher and the mother of six children. Her writings have included articles on education and devotionals forged from her continuing experiences raising six lively children. Contact: 4237 Second St, Riverside, CA 92501. (909) 788-9394. cloud9@pe.net.

Elizabeth Coleman lives in Tumwater, WA with her three sons and husband, Bob. Between wiping peanut butter off walls and pulling weeds, she works as a freelance writer. Contact: dvff75c@prodigy.com.

Peggy Joan Cuthbert and her husband have six grown children and ten grandchildren. She is a church organist and enjoys playing tennis, snow skiing and cross stitching. One of her biggest satisfactions is writing humorous programs for church banquets.

Donella Davis taught junior high for 6 years. She lives in Oklahoma City with her husband, Dr. Mark Davis, and sons, Colten (5) and Kyle (3). Currently, she home schools both boys and is involved in Bible study and her church teen group.

Linda Ross Davis, RN, MBA, is married with two preschoolers. She holds eighteen years experience in health care, has spoken in several major cities, and is interested in Christian-based issues regarding family/career. Contact: lrossdavis@worldnet.att.net.

Pamela F. Dowd is a freelance writer and novelist from East Texas where she lives with her husband and three daughters. On street or treadmill, she enjoys reading and walking simultaneously! Contact: dowpub@juno.com.

Pamela Enderby is the mother of five children. She teaches Bible studies, mentors young moms, and leads an evangelistic prayer group. She enjoys taking long walks with her husband. Contact: gopack@kcter.net.

Marjorie K. Evans is a former school teacher and a freelance writer of many published articles. She enjoys grandparenting, reading, church work, her Welsh corgi, and orchids. She and Edgar have 2 grown sons and 5 grandchildren. Contact: 4162 Fireside Circle, Irvine, CA 92604-2216. (949) 551-5296.

Florence Ferrier lives near Baudette in northern Minnesota. She is a former social worker and now does volunteer work in addition to freelance writing. Her work has appeared in over 40 magazines, plus other publications. Contact: (218) 634-2035.

Ruth Giagnocavo lives in Akron, PA. She is the mother of 7 children and grandmother of 11. Ruth was active in operating a bookstore for twenty years. She writes poetry and has been published in several Christian magazines. Contact: (717) 859-1864.

Florence Grantland is a financial secretary, wife of Ray, mother and grandmother. She is a Bible study teacher and hopes to use her writing and teaching gifts to encourage others. Contact: 1153 Mary's Grove Ch. Rd, Cherryville, NC 28021. (704) 435-0227

Suzanne J. Grenier was born and raised in Salem, MA, and is single and an administrative assistant. She has a BSBA degree and attended Kaleo Bible Institute in Woburn, MA. Contact: 11 Proctor Circle, Peabody, MA 01960. (978) 531-4150.

Denise Hartman Godwin has worked as a journalist and freelance writer. She and her husband spent two years overseas in missions work and hope to work with missionaries again in the future. Contact: DeniseandKerry@juno.com.

Lynell Gray is a freelance writer and elementary school teacher. She has authored professional materials for teachers as well as inspirational articles and poems. Contact: 2867 Balfore St. Riverside, CA. 92506. (909) 788-2638.

Pamela Grubbe and her husband live in the High Sierras where they have been raising their grandson. Mother of four and grandmother of six, she is an avid gardener and hiker. She co-authors a bi-weekly devotional column. Contact: 2215 McCree, Bishop, CA 93514. (760) 873-7839

Colleen Guerrette is recently retired and lives with her husband of 31 years. They have two children. She sings in a gospel trio, plays the piano, and is active in women's ministry. Contact: 1222 Magnolia Ave, #105/209, Corona CA. 91719. andyg@pe.net.

Beverly Hamel went to San Diego, CA from Kansas City, MO via the US Navy and stayed after her enlistment was completed. She's been married to her husband Gary since 1977. She has taught a mixture of Southeast Asian children for over 10 years.

Sharon Hanby-Robie was an ASID designer for 20 years. Now she is an author, speaker, TV personality, and the Creative Director for Starburst Publishers. Contact: sharonrobie@starburstpublishers.com.

Marilyn J. Hathaway writes inspirational messages gleaned from sighting God in marketplace moments. Her family spans four generations of perpetual activity, joy, triumph and tribulation. As a community volunteer, the sources are endless. Contact: 2101 Mariyana Ave, Gallup, NM 87301. (505) 722-9795.

Karen Hayse enjoys being mom to Melinda, foster mom to Nick, and elementary teacher to many. Her daughter's miraculous adoption at age nine inspired Karen's first novel, *Finally Home*, which is being considered for publication. Contact: 5532 Cody, Shawnee, KS 66203

Jan Hoffbauer and her husband, Mike, of 33 years marvel at the blessing of family at the birth of each grandchild. She has over 500 articles published in *The Advertiser-Tribune*. Jan has presented over 70 inspirational talks. Contact: 8395 S SR 231, Tiffin, OH 44883-9245. (419) 927-2729.

Jo Huddleston has written three books: *Amen and Good Morning, God*; *Amen and Good Night, God*; and *His Awesome Majesty*. Her stories and devotionals have appeared in such national magazines as Guideposts and Decision. Jo is a conference workshop speaker.

Michele T. Huey writes feature articles for her local paper, along with writing and editing a weekly devotional column. A former English teacher, she teaches a creative writing class at the Community Center and loves to read. Contact: R.D. 1, Box 112, Glen Campbell, PA 15742. (814) 845-7683.

Kristin Huntley is a full-time wife to husband Wade, and mom to their children Morgan and Ethan. She and her family reside in Overland Park, KS, where they attend Celebration Community Church. Contact: (913) 652-9474. khuntley@yahoo.com

Linda LaMar Jewell is a daughter of the King, wife, mother, writer, encourager, and teacher. She presents workshop on the art of writing letters of appreciation—those "thank you for being you" letters that we all long to receive. Contact: CLASServices, 1-800-433-6633.

Nelda Jones is a freelance writer with poetry, devotionals and articles published in several publications. Mother and grandmother, she received her journalism degree in 1994. Nelda is Media Ministries Director at her church and editor of church newsletter. Contact: Rt 1, Box 81, Edgewood, TX. (903) 896-4885. nfjones@vzinet.com

Kelly King enjoys spending time with her family: Vic, Conner and Courtney. She loves teaching God's Word to teenagers as well as writing and speaking. Contact: 9201 Dena Lane, Oklahoma City, OK 73132. VWKDKING@aol.com

Tina Krause is an award-winning newspaper columnist, public speaker, and freelance writer of over 650 columns, magazine articles, and feature stories. She is the wife of Jim, mother of two adult sons, and grandmother of Ian James. Contact: tinak@netnitco.net.

Marilyn Krebs is originally from California and ministered with her husband in Rochester, NY for ten years. They have five daughters and four grandchildren. She enjoys reading and writing her first novel. Contact: 106 Bluefield Rd, Starr, SC 29684. (864) 296-3732.

Sue Langseth wonders at the beauty of God's creation, and enjoys nothing more than writing about it, painting pictures of it, and digging in it (gardening). Her husband, their three children, dog and cat live happily in Shawnee, KS.

Marilyn Neuber Larson taught fourth grade for thirty years. She is also a conference speaker and author of more than100 stories and articles for both children and adults. Contact: HCR 69, Box 886, Moriarty, NM 87035. (505) 298-1003.

Barbara Lighthizer is a freelance writer, mother, and family historian. Weaving memories of childhood and family experiences into children's stories and devotionals consume most of her free time. Contact: 1749 S.W. Blaine Dr. Aloha, OR 97006. (503) 642-5324. lighthiz@ohsu.edu.

Georgia Curtis Ling is a mom, wife, author, speaker and newspaper columnist. She lives with her husband Phil, their son Phililp and cat, Alice. Contact: 3610 Shore Avenue, Everett, WA 98203.

Gail Gaymer Martin, instructor at Detroit College of Business, is a speaker and writer of six books and numerous articles and short stories. She is a contributing editor for *The Christian Communicator*. Her novel, SEASONS, is a November, 1998 selection of Heartsong Presents. Contact: martinga@aol.com

Jane E. Maxwell, RN, is a freelance writer of inspirational and health articles, devotionals and essays. She is involved with Single Parent and Domestic Violence Prevention Ministries as well as volunteer work for various community agencies. Contact: 1704 Pearl St, Vestal, NY 13850.

Ruth E. McDaniel is a Christian writer, full-time caregiver, witness for the Lord, mother of three, and grandmother of eight.

Kathy Collard Miller is a wife, mother of two adult children, author of over 30 books, and a speaker. She has spoken in over 20 states and three foreign countries. Contact: PO Box 1058, Placentia, CA 92871. (714) 993-2654. Kathyspeak@aol.com.

DiAnn G. Mills lives in Houston, TX with her husband. They are the parents of four sons, ages 19-23, and are active members of Metropolitan Baptist Church. Her writing credits include short stories, articles, devotionals, and a novel published by Heartsong.

Lynn Morrissey, *Words of Life Ministries* founder, professional writer and CLASSpeaker, specializes in workshops on prayer-journaling, spiritual autobiographies, discovering gifts/missions, writing, women's topics, volunteer management, and original speeches. Contact: 155 Linden Ave, St. Louis, MO 63105. (314) 727-8137. morrissey@primary.net

Elaine F. Navarro is a prolific writer whose work has appeared in the pages of the *Ventura County Star*, in Ventura, California. Though a grandmother, Elaine recently completed her college courses and graduated with honors from Ventura College. Contact: eldorado@jetlink.net

Deborah Nell recently moved to Pennsylvania with her husband, Craig, and five-year-old daughter Sophia. They plan on planting a church there with her brother-in-law and sister-in-law. Contact: 340 Nell Road, East Berlin, PA 17316.

Mary Beth Nelson lives with her husband in Clarendon, Texas. She is a retired elementary teacher and freelance writer. Her family consists of four children and nine grandchildren. Her hobbies are music and gardening.

Janie Ness is married to Doug and is a stay-at-home mom to their three teenage children. She has been published in *God's Vitamin "C" for the Hurting Spirit* and writes in her spare time. Contact: 11118 NE 124th Ave., Vancouver, WA 98682. (360) 256-9304.

Carrie Padgett is a wife, homemaker and home educating mother of two teenage daughters. She is active in Women's Ministries and enjoys speaking on marriage and family topics. She is an avid rubber stamper. Contact: 36949 Lexington Ave. Madera, CA 93638. (209) 645-4116.

Sheryl Patterson, wife and mother of three, enjoys writing and gardening in the majestic Sierra mountains where she has lived for 17 years. A graduate of Life Bible College, she enjoys speaking and leading workshops. Contact: 317 Polaris Circle, Bishop, CA 93514. (760) 872-2832

Nancy E. Peterson has been published in several books by Kathy Collard Miller (*God's Vitamin "C" for the Hurting Spirit*, *God's Vitamin "C" for the Spirit of Women*, and *God's Abundance*). Contact: 28626 Tulita Lane, Menifee Valley, CA 92584. (909) 679-5137.

Cora Lee Pless is a wife, mother, writer, and inspirational speaker. Her articles have been published in many periodicals including *Guideposts, Decision,* and *The Christian Reader.* Contact: 127 Overhead Bridge Road, Mooresville, NC 28115. (704) 664-5655. cpless@perigee.net

Karen Poland is a homemaker living in Corpus Christi, Texas. She is the mother of two girls and enjoys reading, writing, birdwatching, and being the wife of a Music Minister in her spare time. You can reach her at KPoland@aol.com.

Margaret Primrose is a retired employee of Nazarene Publishing House who was office editor of *Come Ye Apart* magazine. She has authored two children's books and numerous devotionals and other pieces.

Penny Pierce Rose graduated from Texas Tech University. A wife and mother, she serves in leadership with Women at Calvary, writes Bible study curriculum and speaks at women's conferences and seminars. Contact: 6529 Esther NE, Albuquerque, NM 87109. (505) 823-9416.

Sheri Ryan is a second grade multilingual teacher. She and her husband, Shawn, are celebrating their first year of marriage. Sheri enjoys reading, singing in church, camping and being an aunt. Contact: 1100 N. Placentia #E-28, Fullerton, CA 92831.

Doug Schmidt is a new media consultant who specializes in creative content development. You can reach Doug at Bugsley@aol.com.

Doris Schuchard, previously an early childhood teacher, is a freelance writer for curriculum and family issues. Married and mother of two, she is involved in women's Bible study, teaching VBS, and a Christian writers group. Doris loves reading, crafts and travel.

Merna B. Shank, a secretary at Christian Light Publications (founded by her late husband)

has written numerous poems, short articles, and meditations. She and her adult daughter live together. Contact: 1066 Chicago Avenue, Harrisonburg, VA 22802.

Sherri Shaffer is a wife and mother of two grown children. Her speaking ministry encourages spiritual growth and equips leaders for service. Sherri is a graduate of CLASS (Christian Leaders, Authors and Speakers Seminars), Inc. Contact: 56 Judy St., Corrales, NM 87048. (505) 898-6497.

Linda Evans Shepherd is the author of *Share Jesus Without Fear* with Bill Fay, as well as *Searching for Heather's Heart.* She is a speaker and does women's retreats around the country. Contact: http://www.sheppro.com. (303) 772-2035.

Penny Shoup is a home schooling mother of four children. She enjoys writing inspirational short stories and novels. She loves her husband, horses, and being with children. Contact: 7155 Old Zion Road, Columbia, TN 38401. Bshoup@usit.net.

Claire Sibold is an Associate Professor at Biola University where she teaches in the Education Department. Claire has also taught English, reading, history, and science at the secondary level. Claire and her husband, Jon, have two daughters.

Debra West Smith is a wife and mother of two teenagers. Her work includes books in the *Hattie Marshall Frontier Adventures* series and articles for the Baptist Sunday School Board. Contact: 9158 Arnold Rd., Denham Springs, LA 70726. dlwsmith@juno.com.

Betty Southard is a popular speaker, Bible Teacher and author of *The Grandmother Book* and *One Size Does Not Fit All!* She is also the Minister of Caring for the Hour of Power Television Ministry and serves on the teaching staff of CLASS. Contact: CLASS (800) 433-6633. BettySCA@aol.com

Ronica Stromberg has worked as a newspaper reporter, a marketing assistant, and most recently, an editor for an educational corporation. She now works at home, caring for her son and writing freelance. Contact: 5716 Russell, Mission, KS 66202.

Janice Stroup works part-time in the family business, a jewelry store, teaches piano part time, and writes in her spare time. She lives with her husband, Joe, and three teenage sons, Joshua, Caleb, and Joel. Contact: 403 S. Cedar St., Lincolnton, NC 28092. (704) 735-8851.

Patty Stump is a writer, Bible study teacher, Christian Counselor, and frequent speaker at retreats, conferences, and special events. She communicates messages relevant for today, grounded in Scripture, with humor, encouragement and insights. Contact: PO Box 5003, Glendale, AZ 85312. (602) 979-1441.

Gayle Urban is a freelance writer of poetry, greeting cards, and articles. She began writing at age 7. Gayle is active in local women's ministries and retreats. She delights in encouraging young mothers and sharing hope. She is married and has three teenage sons.

Catherine Verlenden is a membership clerk at The Cloister resort. She is planning to teach English in China, August 1999. Catherine has 4 grown sons, 4 grandchildren and loves to pray, write, and stitch. Contact: 304 Durand Drive #18, Lookout Mountain, GA 30750. (706) 820-1031. cverlenden@juno.com.

Shirley Pope Waite's writing has appeared in over 150 publications and 22 books, including her own devotional book. She teaches memoir writing, leads writers' workshops, and is a co-founder of a local retreat. Shirley resides in Walla Walla, WA.

Lori Wall is a single parent of three children, and the in-house playwright for Pasadena's Exodus Theatre Troupe. She is self-publishing a poetry book to minister to AIDS victims. Contact: PO Box 41-701, Los Angeles, CA 90041. (213) 257-0274.

Kurt C. Ward is President & CEO of Wellspring Consulting Group, Inc., a Christian management consulting firm. He and his wife Karen reside in New Jersey. Contact: 437 Mountain Avenue, North Plainfield, NJ 07062. (908) 668-7830. 2wards@ibm.net.

C. Ellen Watts is writing a humorous book for senior adults from her "Over 60" column in *Herald of Holiness*. Mother of five, grandmother to 15, she writes regularly for Christian and inspirational markets. Contact: 702 Alderwood Ln., Nampa, ID 83651. (208) 466-0813.

Edna B. Welch says her world vision and ministry have been enriched through volunteer teaching of ESL and Citizenship Living Classes to students from more than 20 countries. Contact: 2103 North Price, #105, Fresno, CA 93703.

Kristen Welch is an ordained minister and a youth pastor's wife. She is a freelance writer and is currently working on several writing projects. Kristen and her husband live in Albuquerque, NM with their two golden retrievers. Contact: Kristenwrites@yahoo.com.

Mildred Wenger has written many children's stories in addition to numerous devotionals. She also gives piano and organ lessons. She is married to Daniel and they have five grown children. Contact: 1325 Furnace Hill Road, Stevens, PA 17578.

Shannon Woodward, known for seeing God in ordinary moments, has been published in numerous magazines. She is a teacher, speaker, mother, and Calvary Chapel pastor's wife.

Jenny Yoon is an elementary school teacher working on her Masters in Education at Biola University. She attributes the development of her writing to faithfully writing in her journal the past fifteen years. Contact: (562) 421-8316.

Doris Sterner Young is a retired RN who now devotes her time to freelance writing. She has been published in *Lutheran Women Today*, *God's Abundance*, *Across the Universe*, and *The Christian Communicator*. Contact: 2060 East Cairo Dr., Tempe, AZ 85282. DandGYoung@aol.com.

Other Books By Starburst Publishers
(Partial Listing—full list available upon request)

Why Fret That God Stuff?
Edited by Kathy Collard Miller

Subtitled: *Stories of Encouragement to Help You Let Go and Let God Take Control of All Things in Your Life.* Occasionally, we all become overwhelmed by the everyday challenges of our lives: hectic schedules, our loved ones' needs, unexpected expenses, a sagging devotional life. Why Fret That God Stuff is the perfect beginning to finding joy and peace for the real world! (trade paper)   ISBN 0914984500   **$12.95**

God's Unexpected Blessings
Edited by Kathy Collard Miller

Learn to see the *unexpected blessings* in life. These individual essays describe experiences that seem negative on the surface but are something God has used for good in our lives or to benefit others. Witness God at work in our lives. Learn to trust God in action. Realize that we always have a choice to learn and benefit from these experiences by letting God prove His promise of turning all things for our good.
(hardcover)   ISBN 0914984071   **$18.95**

God's Abundance
Edited by Kathy Collard Miller

This day-by-day inspirational is a collection of thoughts by leading Christian writers such as Patsy Clairmont, Jill Briscoe, Liz Curtis Higgs, and Naomi Rhode. *God's Abundance* is based on God's Word for a simpler, yet more abundant life. Learn to make all aspects of your life—personal, business, financial, relationships, even housework a "spiritual abundance of simplicity." (hardcover)   ISBN 0914984977   **$19.95**

Promises of God's Abundance
Edited by Kathy Collard Miller

The Bible is filled with God's promises for an abundant life. *Promises of God's Abundance* for a More Meaningful Life is written in the same way as the best-selling *God's Abundance.* It will help you discover these promises and show you how simple obedience is the key to an abundant life. Scripture, questions for growth and a simple thought for the day will guide you to a more meaningful life.   ISBN 0914984098   **$9.95**

Revelation—God's Word for the Biblically-Inept
Daymond R. Duck

Revelation—God's Word for the Biblically-Inept is the first in a new series designed to make understanding and learning the Bible as easy and fun as learning your ABC's. Reading the Bible is one thing, understanding it is another! This book breaks down the barrier of difficulty and helps take the Bible off the pedestal and into your hands. (trade paper)   ISBN 0914984985   **$16.95**

Other Books By Starburst Publishers, *continued*

Daniel—God's Word for the Biblically-Inept
Daymond R. Duck

Daniel is the second book in the *God's Word for the Biblically-Inept* series designed to make understanding and learning the Bible easy and fun. *Daniel* is a book of prophecy and the key to understanding the mysteries of the Tribulation and End-Time events. This book is broken down into bite-sized pieces, making it easy to comprehend and incorporate into your daily life. (trade paper)   ISBN 0914984489   **$16.95**

If I Only Knew . . . What Would Jesus Do?
Joan Hake Robie

In what direction are you walking? Is it in His direction? And what about what you're saying? Would He say it? *If I Only Knew. . .* is designed with timely questions, poignant answers, and Scripture. When confronted with a difficult situation, stop—and think *What Would Jesus Do?*

(trade paper)   ISBN 091498439X   **$9.95**

God's Vitamin "C" for the Spirit
Kathy Collard Miller & D. Larry Miller

Subtitled: *"Tug-at-the-Heart" Stories to Fortify and Enrich Your Life.* Includes inspiring stories and anecdotes that emphasize Christian ideals and values by Barbara Johnson, Billy Graham, Nancy L. Dorner, and many other well-known Christian speakers and writers. Topics include: Love, Family Life, Faith and Trust, Prayer, and God's Guidance.

(trade paper)   ISBN 0914984837   **$12.95**

Purchasing Information:
www.starburstpublishers.com

Books are available from your favorite bookstore, either from current stock or special order. To assist bookstore in locating your selection be sure to give title, author, and ISBN #. If unable to purchase from the bookstore you may order direct from STARBURST PUBLISHERS. When ordering enclose full payment plus $3.00 for shipping and handling ($4.00 if Canada or overseas). Payment in U.S. Funds only. Please allow two to three weeks minimum (longer overseas) for delivery. Make checks payable to and mail to: STARBURST PUBLISHERS, P.O. Box 4123, LANCASTER, PA 17604. Credit card orders may also be placed by calling 1-800-441-1456 (credit card orders only), Mon-Fri, 8:30 a.m. to 5:30 p.m. Eastern Standard Time. Prices subject to change without notice. Catalog available for a 9 x 12 self-addressed envelope with 4 first-class stamps.   9-98